The
Life Audit

The Life Audit

A Step-by-Step Guide to Discovering Your Goals and Building the Life You Want

XIMENA VENGOECHEA

CHRONICLE BOOKS
SAN FRANCISCO

Library of Congress Cataloging-in-Publication Data

Names: Vengoechea, Ximena, author.
Title: The life audit : a step-by-step guide to discovering your goals and building the life you want / Ximena Vengoechea.
Description: San Francisco : Chronicle Books, [2024]
Identifiers: LCCN 2024003677 | ISBN 9781797229515 (hardcover)
Subjects: LCSH: Self-actualization (Psychology) | Conduct of life.
Classification: LCC BF637.S4 V45 2024 | DDC 158/.1--dc23/ eng/20240205
LC record available at https://lccn.loc.gov/2024003677

Manufactured in China.

Design by Wynne Au-Yeung.

10 9 8 7 6 5 4 3 2 1

Chronicle books and gifts are available at special quantity discounts to corporations, professional associations, literacy programs, and other organizations. For details and discount information, please contact our premiums department at corporatesales@chroniclebooks.com or at 1-800-759-0190.

Chronicle Books LLC
680 Second Street
San Francisco, California 94107
www.chroniclebooks.com

FOR PAO

INTRODUCTION

UNMOORED
How the Journey Begins

09

PART 1

CONDUCT YOUR LIFE AUDIT
Discover What You Really Want

33

PART 2

UNDERSTAND YOUR LIFE AUDIT
Uncover Personal Insights

83

PART 3

CHART A PATH FORWARD 109

Put Your Life Audit into Action

CONCLUSION

YOU ARE THE ARCHITECT OF YOUR LIFE 171

Stay Grounded in Your Purpose

UNMOORED

How the Journey Begins

Have you ever felt like you were living someone else's life? Like you were meant to be doing one thing, but found yourself doing something else? Or perhaps you have felt overwhelmed by your future, stuck in place and unsure of what to do next. Maybe you have found yourself struggling with where to begin, or have felt lost and uncertain about the path you have chosen. We've all compromised on our dreams at one point or another—or lost the thread of those dreams entirely. But what if we reconnected with our early hopes and wishes for ourselves? What might we change about how we live our lives?

I HAVE LOST
I
HAVE T
L O S T
My
BEARINGS...
I
AM
LOOKING FOR
My
TRUE NORTH

A Crossroads

In 2014, I was at a crossroads. I had just moved to San Francisco from New York as part of an influx of knowledge workers hoping to make it in Silicon Valley. I had tried and failed to get a job out West while in New York, but something told me I would land on my feet if I could just get out there. (The blind self-confidence of being in your twenties!) Shortly after arriving, I got a job at LinkedIn, one of the biggest tech companies in the Bay Area at the time. As a relative newcomer to the tech industry, I had until then only worked at an eight-person start-up in "Silicon Alley" in New York City. Getting the job was more than a relief (my savings would have only lasted so long)—it was a coup.

Yet from the moment I signed the contract, I knew the role came with an expiration date. My job was to quantify customer feedback and funnel it back to the product team to address complaints. My colleagues were deft with spreadsheets and talked CSAT (customer satisfaction) scores in their sleep. But I hated reducing real people's problems to numbers and grew disillusioned that the teams who could fix these problems ever would. The work was also repetitive: The same handful of problems surfaced month after month with little room to explore what a product *could* do or be in the future.

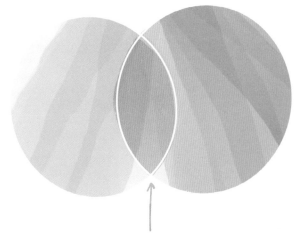

WHAt you LOVE   WHAt you GEt PAID to Do

THE hoLy GRAIL

The more disenchanted I grew with my work, the more I sought inspiration elsewhere. I began to tinker with writing, design, and illustration projects that filled me with joy and a sense of personal momentum. I wondered if I would ever be able to marry doing what I loved with making a living in any meaningful way. There was so much I wanted to do (projects to pursue, skills to acquire, experiences to have)—and even more I might want to do—and I didn't know where to start.

WHAT SHOULD I do NEXT?

The Story of the Life Audit

One afternoon, I sat down to figure it out. I needed to make sense of all the ideas swirling in my head. My usual go-to techniques—writing and talking through my experiences—had come up short. I had too many competing ideas and emotions for journaling: My entries at the time were as messy and confused as I felt. I'd exhausted my friends with angsty conversations about my future. I needed something more concrete and actionable.

I decided to use the tools I knew best. I had just begun to explore a career in user research and would be dedicating 20 percent of my workload to training in this new role. (Spoiler alert: I would do this for the next decade of my career.) I decided to borrow a page from the user research book.

What's a User Researcher?

User researchers seek to understand people's needs, motivations, feelings, behaviors, and perceptions. Sometimes these things are evident at the surface, but tuning into these things often takes a little bit of work, which is where I come in. Researchers like me must be part therapist, part coach, part detective—a facilitator, a conduit, as well as a vessel for helping people uncover hidden needs and desires.

For example, if I am conducting a study about vacation planning, I might learn about people's vacation-planning process and approach. Certain needs will be obvious: People may need more time or money than they have to plan a vacation they'll love. Other wants and needs will be less obvious: People may want a vacation without their family but feel too guilty to plan a solo trip. They may feel ashamed that they don't make as much money as their peers and can't spend on dinners out in the same way. These deeper needs and desires emerge thanks to the skillful questioning and data analysis of user researchers.

As a budding user researcher, I knew the power of sticky notes and a good cluster analysis. Brainstorming, mapping data, looking for themes and patterns, and eventually synthesizing them into insights were becoming my bread and butter. They were what I was being trained to do every time I ran a research study: data in, insights out. Why not apply this technique to my own life? Using only sticky notes and a permanent marker, I charted out my many what-ifs and if-onlys and systematically sorted through them.

When a researcher runs a brainstorm, everything is deliberate. We use sticky notes because they aren't precious, and neither are our ideas. We use thick permanent markers to help us capture the root of an idea, its core, without getting bogged down in details. (The larger the marker, the less room on the sticky note, the simpler the idea.) We remind participants that no idea is too small, no idea too silly. We create a judgment-free zone to encourage blue-sky thinking. I kept this in mind as I captured ideas and made my way through my stack of sticky notes, following the *design thinking* rule of one idea per note. No wish was too grandiose, no desire too embarrassing to admit. All ideas were good ideas.

An hour later, I had generated 121 ideas. I wanted to visit all seven continents (five down, two to go). To call my parents more often. To change careers. To write a book. And much, much more. I had uncovered hopes and dreams I had never dared to say aloud.

Then, it was time to move on to *affinity mapping*, or grouping data into themes. With instant visual clarity, I could see how many of my wishes and desires were about career or family or creative pursuits. I looked for other patterns, identifying new themes. Looking closer, I saw that each group was related to at least one other (life is too complicated to be neat and tidy). So I kept going, looking for connections from group to group. When I looked at things this way, I could see that some of the skills I wanted to acquire stemmed from values I held dear. So many of the things I wanted to do—like writing, public speaking, illustrating—were tied to a core value around the importance of knowledge-sharing and peer mentorship. As I synthesized my data, insights began to emerge, and for the first time, I could clearly see what it was I *really* wanted. There was a hierarchy to my wants and needs too: I had a sense of when to do what, which made the results invigorating, not over-whelming. I published a quick write-up online in the hopes that it might help others (knowledge-sharing, of course). Thus, the life audit—an exercise in self-reflection to help individuals uncover their values, desires, and life goals—was born.

My idea of "spring-cleaning for the soul" struck a chord. Friends and strangers alike shared photos of their own life audits on social media. Organizations conducted life audits as team-bonding and vision-building exercises. Readers sent heartfelt emails about their experiences. Suddenly, the media took an interest, spreading the gospel of the life audit.

This simple weekend activity set my life in motion in ways I could not have anticipated. I was profiled in *Fast Company* and asked to become a contributor. A few years later, a literary agent saw my work in *Fast Company* and offered me representation. Our partnership would turn into three books (and counting), including the one you're holding right now. A decade since my first life audit, I have accomplished much of what I set out to do, including writing books, and I return to it annually to check in with myself to see what still feels relevant and what new dreams and desires have cropped up. Years after doing their own life audits, I still get emails from people whose audits have helped them to reconnect with their desires and make space for meaningful change.

Many people say the life audit helped them find clarity in their lives. Some realized they were in denial about their marriage and had been ignoring their gut instinct for too long. Others learned they were people pleasers and reflected on how this might be getting in the way of their dreams. Still others finally saw how unhappy they were in their careers. Whatever the revelation, these personal insights helped life auditors put meaningful changes in motion. From developing their instinct or setting more boundaries, to getting divorced, changing careers, or prioritizing more family time, the life audit played an important role in revealing hidden desires while encouraging them to pursue long-standing ones.

And they didn't just discover what was missing but what was working well too: They realized they had a strong support network already, or were showing up as their true and authentic selves, or had achieved more than they had given themselves credit for. These insights led them to double down on fulfilling relationships, make the time and space to celebrate their achievements, and appreciate their true selves.

LIFE AUDIT.

(noun)

AN EXERCISE in SELF-REFLECTION that helps you CLEAR the COBWEBS of noisy, EXTERNAL goALS and CURRENT distRACTIONS, and REVISIT OR UNCOVER the REAL themes and CORE VALUES that DRIVE and INSPIRE you. ALSO KNOWN AS SPRING-CLEANING for the SOUL.

How a Life Audit Works

The Life Audit is an invitation to rediscover your values, passions, and dreams. Together, we'll uncover what you desire, figure out what's holding you back, and develop an action plan for putting changes into place and living a life that honors your purpose and aligns with your values. We'll use design thinking principles and user research techniques to design a solution that is based on real needs, motivations, perceptions, and emotions—yours. Like good user researchers, we'll analyze, interrogate, and probe deeper as our answers come in, ensuring that we're getting to the root of our desires—the real wants deep within us, not the things we think (or have been told) we should want.

The life audit is a safe space for dreaming big, a path to kick-start dreams previously on hold, and an honest gut check for honoring our values and desires every day. It is a system to help you prioritize your goals and turn personal insights into action.

WHAT TO EXPECT

The life audit answers essential questions like:

- What are my goals?

- What are my values?

WHAT WOULD BRING ME JOY IN LIFE?

- Am I spending my time in line with these goals and values?

- What's getting in my way?

- How nourishing are my relationships?

- Do I have the right people in my corner to realize my goals, aspirations, and intentions?

The questions so many of us have about how to find our purpose, live a good life, start over, or simply try something new are questions I've explored not just as a writer, parent, spouse, friend, and person in the world, but also as a researcher. Although I was trained primarily to help companies build products, services, and experiences that meet real people's needs, I have come to find my research skills to be very valuable in my personal life as well. It's this training that led me to the life audit and the book you're holding in your hands now. Throughout the book, you'll learn more about this training, how it fits into the life audit practice, and what makes it such a valuable set of tools for facilitating introspection and finding clarity and direction.

Since its original publication, many readers have written to me asking for additional guidance to make their life audits come true. In this new update, you'll find new illustrations, inspiration, and a special section on how to put your life audit into action. You'll also find actionable prompts to help you turn

your life audit into reality, without feeling overwhelmed. I'll
guide you through questions like:

- What should I do next?

- What is a priority now versus later?

- What resources (people, skills, things) do I need
  to make progress?

You'll also find new exercises and journaling prompts to help
you process your experience and to capture learnings and reflections throughout the journey. Most important, you will have a
chance to reconnect with yourself and experience self-discovery
and self-knowledge.

The work of introspection during this process can be thrilling
and rewarding but also challenging. You may find that admitting your desires is uncomfortable. You may feel a tension
between what you really want from your life and what you've
been told all your life that you ought to want from it or believe
you should want from it. You may feel conflicted between
your true desires and your real responsibilities. This is normal.
See what comes up for you and keep an open mind. Accept it.
Respect it. Embrace it. Your life audit is your personal road map
to living the life you want. Now is the time for self-discovery.

HOW am I DOING?

WHERE Am I GOING?

WHAT'S IMPORTANT NOW THAT WASN'T BEFORE!

How to Use This Book

This book is your complete A to Z guide for conducting your very own life audit. It is designed to be read in order; you might get a little lost if you try to jump around. The book is organized into three sections:

In Part 1, we surface our hopes and dreams. If you are feeling confused, stuck, unmotivated, or unclear about what you want, Part 1 will be particularly useful for you.

In Part 2, we make meaning of the desires and ideals we have discovered—and by extension, of ourselves.

In Part 3, we get tactical and ready for action. If you know what you want but have trouble turning desire into action or feel overwhelmed by your ambitions and are uncertain about where to start, Part 3 will be especially valuable for you. Each part works hand in hand so that by the end of the book you can go from insights to action.

You can conduct your life audit all in one go, or pace yourself and complete it section by section over time. Some people find themselves in an adrenaline rush of clarity and exhilaration and finish in a single sitting, while others benefit from taking breaks. It depends on your stamina (and on how much autonomy you have over your schedule day-to-day). Personally, I have found that taking breaks and letting things marinate at key points can be very helpful. If you find yourself feeling stuck on how to make a change or what to prioritize, or are unsure if you've been honest with yourself in your list of goals and desires, taking a break gives your subconscious a chance to problem solve. Taking a walk around the block, setting aside an afternoon to think about something totally different, or escaping into your favorite fictional world for a bit can help. If you prefer to complete your life audit piece by piece, I recommend following the structure of the book and completing Parts 1, 2, and 3 in separate sessions. Or just audit until you're tired and pick it up again the next day.

If something does not resonate with you, feel free to adapt it to your liking. For example, if I suggest finding a quiet, solo space for brainstorming your deepest desires but you need music and activity to get the creative juices flowing, add your own twist with a playlist. If you are naturally self-motivated and already have a prioritization framework that works for you, leverage it. If you have a journaling practice that allows you to go deeper, use it. Although I have refined this method over the years, you may need something slightly different. What's most important is that you give yourself a chance to self-reflect, to get to know yourself, and to allow your deepest desires to make themselves known. Only in knowing what we want can we begin to get there.

Why we audit

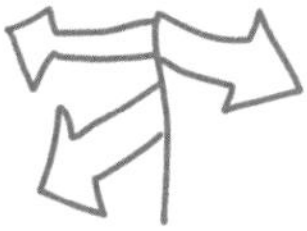

We are at a crossroads

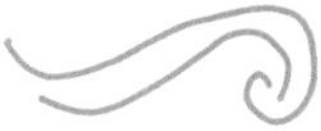

We are ready for a change

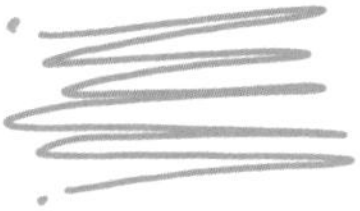

We are overwhelmed by our ambitions

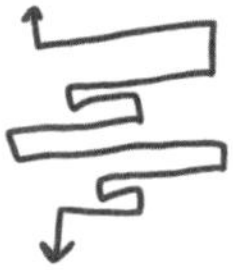

We are unsure of what we want

We are seeking inspiration

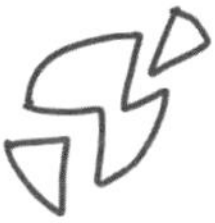

We want to feel complete

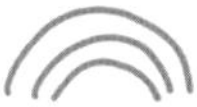

We want a life beyond our jobs

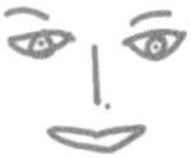

We want to get to know ourselves

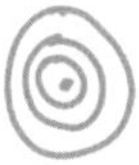

We are seeking focus

THE BEST TIME FOR A LIFE AUDIT

When should you conduct your life audit? Many people find the life audit to be especially useful during moments of transition and uncertainty. When we face a personal crossroads such as a career change, geographic move, pivotal birthday, parenthood, school graduation, retirement, or other milestone, clarity and direction can be an encouraging balm. Others plan life audits for the end of the year, when we are in an introspective mindset. It's a great time to reflect on life audits past and to appreciate how far we've come.

Sometimes it's obvious to us why we are called to dig deeper, but at other times it's not. Ultimately, you should conduct your life audit whenever the spirit moves you. When you're seeking clarity or wanting to reconnect with yourself. When you're in need of direction and encouragement. When you're ready to dig deep into what it is you want from this life and what's getting in your way. You needn't wait for a special date or occasion to think more deeply about your life. When you can find the time, space, and mental energy to answer meaningful questions about your life, the moment is right. Now that you've arrived, let's get started.

PART 1

CONDUCT YOUR LIFE AUDIT

Discover What You Really Want

Prepare • One Hundred Sticky Notes in an Hour • Map Your Wishes • Identify Core Values and Intentions • Top Five Activities • Five People

In this section, I'll take you through the step-by-step process of conducting your life audit. You'll learn how to set yourself up for a successful life audit and begin your journey of self-discovery.

Prepare

Before you get started, you'll need to prepare a few things: your materials, your space, and yourself. As you'll see in the pages to follow, the most important ingredient is you—so take the time to make sure you're ready to be open, to explore, to self-reflect, to surprise, and to delight yourself.

PREPARE YOUR MATERIALS

You'll only need a few materials to get started, but it is important to use the *right* materials. Using the right tools helps create a safe space to be imperfect and daring in our self-discovery. The wrong tools—overly rigid, too neat—can discourage us by suggesting perfection is needed when raw, half-shaped ideas are best. To that end, I've listed the necessary tools below, each deliberately chosen for optimal results.

- Sticky notes

- Permanent markers

- A bare wall or floor space you can take over for a few hours

- A journal or notebook and a pen

It's very important to use analog, or physical, tools—not digital ones. Why? Using a thick permanent marker and a standard 3-by-3-inch sticky note ensures that you don't overthink each wish—you can only write what fits onto the note, preventing you from overcomplicating things. Plus, sticky notes are meant to be tossed aside—they're not precious or meant to be permanent, which can be freeing as we brainstorm. It will also make sorting and categorizing your wishes much easier later on.

As tempting as it may be to go digital, you won't get the desired outcome if you swap in Google Docs, Trello, or your Notes app for sticky notes and a permanent marker. Switching to a Google doc or other digital tool gives you too much space to overanalyze and overedit your wishes. Digital tools can also be a huge distraction. Even with the best of intentions and ironclad willpower, our devices can pull us out of the moment. Don't battle notifications, twitchy fingers, and auto-play while you conduct your life audit. Give yourself a shot at real momentum and put your phone and other devices out of sight for best results.

Scrappy Process, Scrappy Materials

Early in my career as a user researcher, I got some excellent advice from a manager: If your insights are half-baked, don't make a fancy presentation out of them or people will expect more than they should. Instead, use tools that show it is a work in progress. Signal the stage of work you're in through the materials you choose. I find the same lesson holds for completing your life audit, even with an audience of only one. We want to use tools that encourage imperfection because that's what life is.

PREPARE YOUR SPACE

User researchers utilize whiteboards, walls, and large foam core boards to analyze and synthesize ideas—in other words, we use large surfaces where we can take up a *lot* of space to think and rethink information, map ideas out this way and that, and eventually turn data into insights. If you happen to have a foam core board or a whiteboard at home, feel free to repurpose it for your life audit. But since most of us don't have access to these materials, here are some simple ideas for optimally preparing your space for your life audit:

- **Clear some space.** I recommend using a large wall or floor for your sorting. Of the two, I prefer using a wall when possible—you don't have to clean it up immediately, and it's easier to leave up for a few days while you mull things over (no need to walk around it!). You also won't wind up with a neck cramp from staring at the floor all day. But either will do the trick. Having ample space will be especially useful in the sorting and categorizing phase of your life audit.

- **Get some privacy.** The life audit is a personal exercise— it's about architecting *your* life, after all. For this reason, you might find that you are most comfortable doing your life audit alone. (For tips and tricks on how to make this a group activity or team-bonding exercise, see the FAQs on page 179.) Taping a simple "Privacy please" sign on your door can deter roommates, spouses, or children from interrupting. If home interruptions are insurmountable (I get it!), grab your stickies, markers, and this book and head to a coffee shop, coworking space, park, or other space in which you can work quietly and anonymously on your life audit. Although you won't be able to spread out and reorganize your wishes, you can at least complete the generative parts of your life audit in this shared space. Just be sure it's a place free enough of distractions where you can get some good thinking and reflecting done.

- **Incorporate generative accessories (optional).**
  Generative accessories are those things that help us generate ideas and create space for self-reflection. If you have personal, go-to accessories that help you get in the zone for introspection, now is the time to pull them out. For instance, for some of us, having music in the background can help us get in the right state of mind, while for others, it's a distraction. You can mark this time with a ritual of lighting a candle or incense if that is meaningful to you, or skip it if that feels too woo-woo. You can wear your coziest slippers and get comfy with a mug of tea, or go barefoot and pace as you go, as I did during my first life audit.

PREPARE YOURSELF

Being the architect of your life is exciting—this is a chance to rediscover what you love and want and reconnect with yourself. But it can also be daunting: Who knows what you will find? You can mentally prepare yourself for what comes next with a few essential ingredients:

- **An open mind:** Keeping an open mind means being receptive to whatever comes up, observing and accepting it even if a wish surprises you, embarrasses you, unsettles you, or makes you feel very vulnerable. Be honest with yourself: Admit the deep desires; ignore the societal, cultural, and familial obligations that tell you what you *should* want; and embrace your truest, most honest wishes instead. This is the most important ingredient to making your life audit a success. Now is not the time to chastise yourself for your wishes or to talk yourself out of them. When a wish comes up that you feel uncertain or uncomfortable about, simply acknowledge: *That is a wish I have.*

- Self-compassion: As you go through your life audit, you may feel any number of emotions: hope, optimism, joy, exhilaration, fear, shame, regret, or even guilt. It can be tempting to judge ourselves for our choice of goals as well as for our progress, or lack thereof—to see all that we want to do and reprimand ourselves for not having done more already. But the life audit is ultimately about clarity, not judgment. Do your best to offer yourself self-compassion about the choices, decisions, and responsibilities that have led you to where you are today. When you feel the itch to be self-critical, stop and ask yourself what you would say to a friend. Would you offer them criticism at this moment of vulnerability, or extend understanding, compassion, and encouragement?

- Curiosity and delight: Allow your life audit to bring not just moments of clarity but also joy, glee, and excitement. Get curious about what comes up for you. Delight in its newness. Notice when you are surprised and appreciate those moments. Pay attention to what energizes you. Let your audit reignite your passions and raise new questions. Curiosity is the best partner for exploring.

PRACTICING SELF-COMPASSION SOUNDS LIKE...

WHAT INFORMATION DID I HAVE AT THE TIME?

WAS IT THE RIGHT DECISION GIVEN WHAT I KNEW THEN?

WAS I DOING THE BEST I COULD?

One Hundred Sticky Notes in an Hour

Now we are ready to uncover our innermost desires, wishes, and aspirations. By the end of this section, you'll have a glimpse of what it is you want, how you wish to live your life, the values you want to live by, and the hopes and dreams you hold for yourself.

BRAINSTORM

The first step is simple: Set aside an hour and, using one hundred sticky notes, write a single wish on each one. These can be any kind of wish or goal you'd like—no wish is too big or too small. (I use the words *wish*, *goal*, *intention*, and *desire* interchangeably here because our innermost wants can take many different forms.) Keep going until you reach one hundred or run out of wishes.

Here are a few suggestions to help you dig deep and wish for what your heart really wants.

Wish Like No One's Watching

As you compile your list, be sure to stay true to yourself. Now is the time to shed others' expectations of you and tune into your

I WISH

own desires. Make each wish true and honest to *you*—not to others. If you notice that your wishes feel more like obligations or "shoulds" rather than true desires, or if they feel forced or as if they belong to someone else, take a step back, set them aside, and start over with more honesty in your heart. Allow your hopes and dreams to emerge without fear of whether or not you can make them come true and without judging whether you "ought" to be wishing for something else.

When I ran my first life audit back in 2014, I had a lot of goals: To do more public speaking. To fill my passport but know where my home was. To make something people love. Each desire was an important data point for understanding myself.

"SHOULD" WISHES	TRUE WISHES
HAVE a KID	WORK with KIDS
BECOME a LAWYER	BECOME an ARTIST
TRAVEL	NEST
MAKE MY PARENTS HAPPY	MAKE MYSELF HAPPY
GET PROMOTED	SWITCH CAREERS
STUDY MORE	PLAY MORE

Take Your Time

Somewhere around thirty to forty sticky notes, you might find you've run out of wishes. That might even bring you some relief: The fewer goals, the more within reach, right? Before you pump the brakes on wishing, pause for a moment. Give yourself a few minutes to see whether anything else comes up or if you really are finished. You might get a second wind and uncover an urge to keep going.

Of course, you needn't force yourself to get to one hundred wishes, or stick out a full hour of wishing time (or if you're bursting with ideas, to limit yourself to one hundred wishes within an hour). But it's a good idea to include a small introspective pause in your process. The number is not what matters. What matters is that you take the time to allow your desires to come to the surface.

Why a Brainstorm?

In user research, brainstorms help teams gather wild and inventive ideas and imagine the future of a product. They can also help participants navigate a thorny situation and chart a path forward. In our case, we want to give ourselves permission to dream the dreamiest dreams and wish the wildest wishes. We want to allow ourselves to be honest about what we want, even if it feels uncomfortable. This is our blue skies, anything-is-possible, all-ideas-are-good-ideas brainstorm. Capturing our ideas on sticky notes is a way to "think out loud" on paper.

Strategies for Getting Unstuck

If you find you're having trouble getting your thoughts on paper, the following techniques can help:

- **Write for a few minutes with your nondominant hand.** Sometimes we need to slow things down to let ideas emerge. One way to do this is to write a handful of wishes with your nondominant hand. If you're a lefty, see if you can get a few wishes out with your right hand, and vice versa. This simple act of doing things differently can unlock our thinking and help us get unstuck.

- **Edit later.** Any author will tell you that a blank page is much harder to work with than a full one. Get all your ideas out there, even if they make you cringe or are not fully articulated. Write down any idea that comes to mind whether or not you think you might toss it later. Just the seed of an idea is worth getting on paper—you can deepen it later on. Simply getting something out on paper can be generative and build momentum.

- Add a time constraint. Setting a timer to brainstorm for just a few minutes can lower the pressure to generate ideas and get you unblocked. Start with five minutes and see what happens. If five minutes feels too stressful, drop it to one or two. Once your timer chimes, there usually will be one of two outcomes: You'll find you either want to keep going or scrap what you've come up with. *Either outcome is useful.* Why? You now have something to work with and react to. If you don't like the wishes you've outlined in the allotted time, why not? If they're not true to you, what would make them more honest? Whose voice is getting in the way? (Capitalism? Your parents?) If you like what you've uncovered, great! Use this as inspiration to keep going. Whether you like the ideas or not, in just five minutes you have proven to yourself that there *are* ideas, desires, goals, and aspirations ready to break through to the surface. Now, keep going. Scrap the timer and experiment with longer increments if you're ready, or keep it and brainstorm in shorter bursts if that's best for you.

- Take a break. If you're having trouble generating ideas, take a break to recharge your thinking. I recommend taking a walk, reading through old journals, doing some jumping jacks, or even taking a shower. (Nothing gets the old noggin going quicker than letting our minds wander while we shampoo.) Don't go on social media, send a bunch of emails, or plop yourself in front of Netflix. Those types of "breaks" tend to tamp down inspiration and distract us. You can even come back to this tomorrow. Sometimes it's best to let things breathe.

- **Look inward.** You might think that having another voice in the mix can help you get unstuck. Maybe you want a sounding board or some encouragement that your ideas are good and meaningful or that you're on the right track. But it's best to protect your ideas at this stage; they might be too fragile for input from others. If you are seeking direction, look inward instead.

Map Your Wishes

Look at you, with all those wishes! Congratulations on getting them out there. Our next step is to begin to make sense of our raw data—the sometimes repetitive, sometimes only semi-articulated goals and wants you've identified. We'll map our wishes across multiple axes to get deep insight into what we want and when we want it.

NOTES from the FIELD

Affinity Mapping

When user researchers work with large amounts of data, they need a systematic way to help them sort through and make meaning of it. Otherwise, it's easy to quickly get overwhelmed and fall into "analysis paralysis." *Affinity mapping* is a handy user research technique that can help you find the signal in the noise. It is deceptively simple: User researchers look for patterns and themes in the data and then group the data accordingly. They map data into themes according to affinity, meaning by how closely related a data point is to another. Then they do it again, and again, poking holes at previous groupings, looking for clearer and stronger connections, refining existing groupings, until they are satisfied with their mapping. Affinity mapping can help you make sense of your life audit in much the same way.

GROUP LIKE WITH LIKE

The easiest place to start is by grouping your wishes by similarity. For example, let's say one of your goals is to start a family, another is to keep in touch with your siblings, and another is to put together a family tree, plus do an audio project to capture your parents' voices. These could all be grouped together under the theme of family.

To group your themes, grab a fresh sticky note and write down the group category, then plop your wish stickies underneath the group name like so:

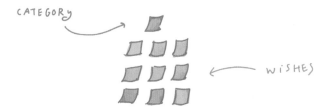

In most cases, it will be fairly obvious how to group your wishes. Especially in this first pass, follow your intuition as to how they should be grouped.

If you're having trouble getting started, try thinking about the following:

- *What* the wish is about: Is there a topic, category, community, or idea that keeps coming up?

- *Who* the wish is about: Do the same characters appear across certain wishes? For example, family, friends, coworkers, and so on.

- *Where* the wish might occur: Is there an obvious setting that these wishes are tied to? For example, a university or school setting, an office or workplace, a gym, a church, a community center, a home?

Given what you learn, you might find that a handful of categories cover all of your wishes—or that *many* categories are needed to make sense of your desires. Either outcome is fine at this stage.

Here are just a few examples of themes that might come up, but there are many others. None of these are prerequisites.

THEMES to help you GET STARTED

LEISURE time

COMMUNITY

FAMILY

HEALtH

SPIRITUALITY

CREATIVE PURSUITS

ADVENTURE

RELATIONSHIPS

CAREER

EXPLORE NEW THEMES

Now that you have a bird's-eye view of your wishes, you can look at whether the themes you've uncovered are the best groupings to give you insight into what you want. Some of your first groupings, culled from your intuition, may remain the strongest. Some may dissolve completely, absorbed by other groups.

For example, let's return to the hypothetical goals you have grouped under the theme of family: starting a family, keeping in touch with your siblings, putting together a family tree, and doing an audio project to capture your parents' voices. These could all be grouped together under the theme of family, as we did on our first pass. But they could also be broken up into two different themes: family (starting a family and keeping in touch with your siblings) and creative projects or hobbies (putting together a family tree and doing an audio project about your parents).

As you return to your wishes, consider the following questions to help you explore new themes where necessary:

- Are my categories porous? Do they overlap with other categories? Is this helpful or confusing? What might a less porous, more defined set of categories look like?

- How specific are my labels? Do I find it useful or over-whelming to be specific?

- Which categories compete with each other? In what way? What makes them different from each other? Is there a new, overarching category that describes this difference? Is it useful to recategorize in this way?

- Which categories feel aligned or connected to each other, like sister themes? In what ways are they related to each other? Is there a new, overarching category that describes this alignment? Is it useful to recategorize in this way?

You'll know a new grouping or theme is best when the relationship between the items feels strong, not tenuous. (If you're not sure, follow your intuition.) As a rule of thumb, if you have more than fifteen categories, this is likely a sign that your categories are too specific; if you have only three, your categories are likely too broad. With each round of refinement, you will get a clearer picture of what it is you're truly after.

EXPERIMENT WITH DIFFERENT DIMENSIONS

At this point, if you are happy with your categories, great! But if you could use more clarity, keep refining them. You can do this by experimenting with different dimensions as you group your wishes.

For example, in my initial mapping, I had one giant category labeled *health*. But when I took a closer look, I realized I could break this category down further across three additional dimensions: physical health, financial health, and spiritual health. In the end, although it was useful to see the big-picture takeaway—that I wanted to feel healthy—it was even more useful to discover the *kind* of healthy I needed.

Here are some examples of dimensions you might consider experimenting with:

- Instead of "relationships," ask yourself whether these relationships are familial, romantic, friend, collaborator, competitor, etc.

- Instead of "hobbies," ask yourself whether these hobbies are active, passive, solo, group, skills-based, arts-based, or if they live on any other continuum.

- Instead of "professional," try exploring dimensions like skills-building, community-building, or career advancement.

Sometimes you will find that your umbrella category is more useful than slicing wishes by specific dimension, but at other times the opposite will be true. The only way to know for certain is to experiment and try things in more than one way to find what fits best.

TALLY UP YOUR WISHES

Count the number of wishes in each group. Write down this number on the sticky note you used to label each category. (If you are more of a linear thinker, you can make a list of the themes you've identified and tally the number of wishes per theme.)

CAREER (4)   SpiRituALity (7)   LOVE (3)

Once you have counted up the wishes in each group, place each grouping in order from lowest to highest according to the number of wishes to see where the heat is. You'll be able to tell which themes are most popular based on the size of each group of stickies.

LOVE (3)   CAREER (4)   SPIRITUALITY (7)

Pay attention to which group includes the most wishes and how you feel about it. You may feel excited, intimidated, overwhelmed, embarrassed, inspired, empowered, or even surprised by what you've discovered. Look at your smallest grouping too. Are these in line with your expectations? Do they feel like an accurate reflection of who you are? Remember that your life audit is a snapshot in time—a reflection of what you want *today*. That might change over the years, or it might hold steady and true over time.

Do not feel pressure to add more wishes to areas you feel you "should" be focused on; take note of your true "wants" instead. Let it be what it needs to be, which is, above all, honest.

We'll spend time unpacking these results further in Part 3, but for now, simply tally things up and notice your response to the final count. This count will prove handy later on as we turn our personal "data" into self-knowledge and insights.

A life's worth of wishes,

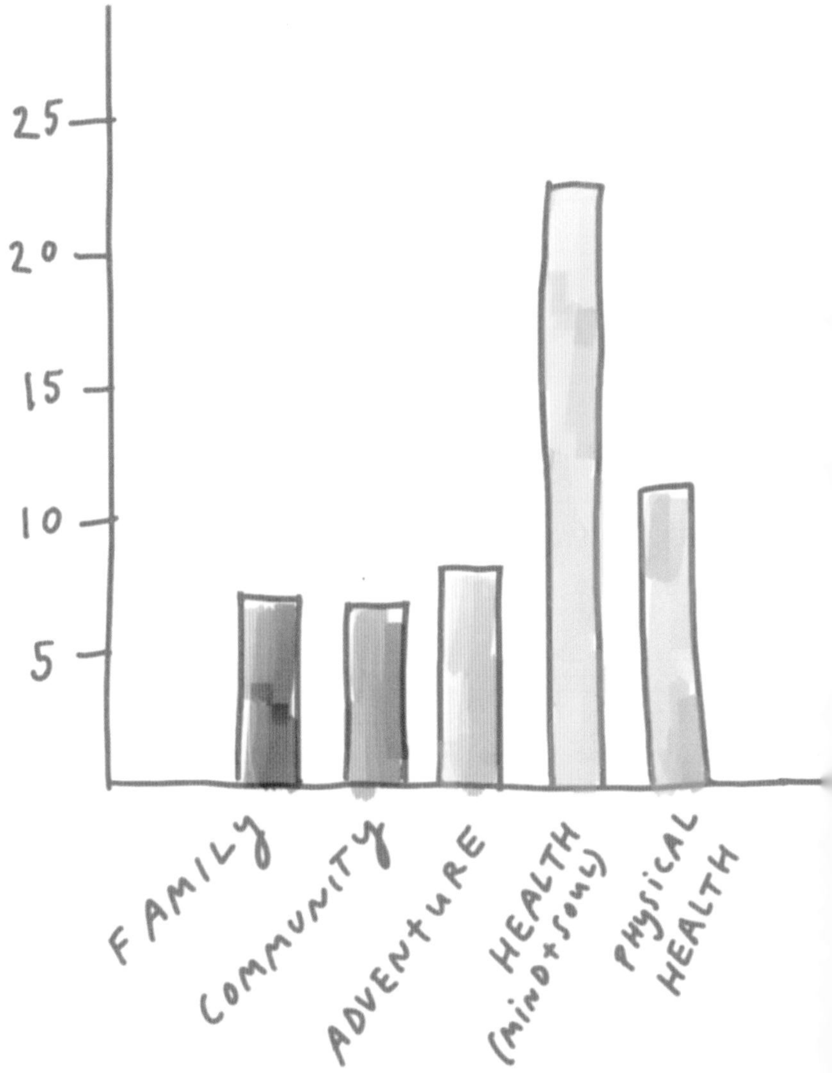
25
20
15
10
5
FAMILY
COMMUNITY
ADVENTURE
HEALTH (MIND+SOUL)
PHYSICAL HEALTH

SORTED BY TYPE

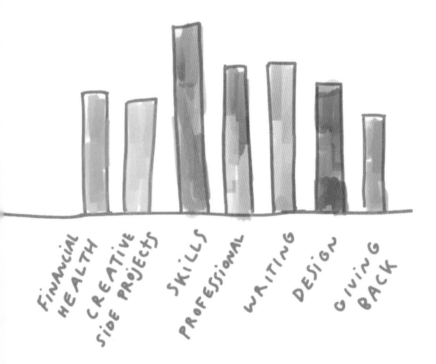

FINANCIAL HEALTH CREATIVE SIDE PROJECTS SKILLS PROFESSIONAL WRITING DESIGN GIVING BACK

Identify Core Values and Intentions

As you take another look at your wishes, you may notice that some feel different in nature than others. You may have a mix of very tangible goals ("make $100k"), grandiose wishes ("become a bestselling author"), and wishes that exist on a more individual level ("be more patient"). This last category of wishes includes the ideals, values, and intentions for how you want to live your daily life. These include beliefs we hold about what it means to be a good person and to live a good life, as well as intentions for living or behaving a certain way. This might include things like "to support my family" or "to never take no for an answer." Often, our intentions are shaped by a deeper core value or conviction, such as a belief in filial piety and a responsibility to our parents or that perseverance can defeat the odds.

Because our core values and intentions shape how we move through the world, they will also often cut across many categories in our life audit. You may see values crop up in each of your overarching themes in different ways.

Here are some examples of wishes that might have surfaced in your life audit in the form of intentions, along with examples of the deeper core values they might represent:

INTENTION	CORE VALUE
TO SLOW DOWN	PEACE, CALM, PATIENCE, REST
TO BE KIND	KINDNESS, COMPASSION
TO BE MORE GENEROUS	EMPATHY, GENEROSITY
TO BE A GOOD FRIEND	COMMUNITY, LOYALTY
TO BE THERE FOR my FAMILY	DUTY, FAMILY, TRADITION
TO SHARE my LEARNINGS	TEACHING, MENTORSHIP, COACHING
TO BE MORE VULNERABLE	INTIMACY, SELF-AWARENESS
TO BE MY OWN ADVOCATE	SELF-RESPECT, SELF-WORTH
TO TRUST my INTUITION	SELF-CONFIDENCE, FAITH, INNER WISDOM

I WANT TO

TRUST MY INTUITION

BE A GOOD FRIEND

BE GENEROUS

SLOW DOWN

TALLY UP YOUR VALUES AND INTENTIONS

Take a moment to identify the core values and intentions in your life audit. Draw a small heart in the corner of any wishes that fit this category. When you finish, notice where these values arise. Are any themes rich in core values? Poor in them? Do not change any wishes or groupings at this time. Simply notice where your values are surfacing and any feelings you are having in response. We will look at our values and intentions in more detail in Part 3.

Now is a great time to stretch your body, roll out your neck, and shake your hands out before moving to the next section.

Top Five Activities

In the previous step, we surfaced our wishes and desires. But now comes a chaser of reality: Are we using our time in alignment with the themes and intentions that matter most to us, or not? In this section, we'll look at how we spend our time, and whether that's taking us toward or away from our goals.

WHERE DOES THE TIME GO?

Take a minute to jot down the five to ten activities that you spend the most time on, on average. This is going to give you a quick glimpse at what I call your *pointless to purposeful ratio*—or how much time you spend on things that are meaningful and aligned with your life audit versus all the other stuff that can easily fill a day. List them in the order of which activities are most time-consuming (on average), or draw them in proportion to how much time you spend on them. Here's what mine looks like:

WHERE DOES THE TIME GO?

CHILD+
PET
CARE

WRITING

EXERCISE

READING

LIFE
ADMIN

DRAWING

PODCASTS

SOCIALIZING

It's crucial to be honest here. You might not like what you find, but you can't fix things if you ignore the problem. Or you might love what you find, in which case, well done! Whether you feel you have the time you need or not nearly enough, it's helpful to get a snapshot of how you typically spend your time.

Know, too, that your top hits reflect a specific moment in time—that is, right now. The first time I conducted a life audit, back when I was child-free, partner-free, and dog-free, my results looked very different than they do today. Unsurprisingly, they've changed a lot since then.

Your personal top activities are a reflection of your priorities, circumstances, and interests—and those can sometimes be at odds with each other but may evolve over time.

Once you've finished compiling your top time-consuming activities, review your list and notice your response. Are you happy with your list? Surprised by it? How close—or far—is it from where you want to be?

TIME SPENT THEN

DESIGNING

SOCIALIZING

EXERCISING

WRITING

WORK

SKETCHING

TIME SPENT NOW

CHILD +
PET
CARE

WRITING

LIFE
ADMIN

EXERCISE

READING

SOCIALIZING

DRAWING

PODCASTS

FREE TIME

You might have noticed that in my top activities—and likely yours as well—there's a big ole chunk of time dedicated to work. Whether your version of work is showing up at an office, going to school, or taking care of your kids, chances are this is your most time-consuming regular activity, and more or less immovable; it's a big responsibility, and you might not have much autonomy over it. For most of us, there is a large portion of our time that is non-fungible.

Some of us will want to include this non-fungible chunk in our calculus of whether or not we are spending our time in line with our goals and values. We will want to assess whether our work is aligned with our purpose and mission in life. But for others, a job is just a job—not a vocation or calling—and its main purpose is to fund and support *other* things we find meaningful. This is your call.

Whether or not you include this in your overall assessment, you can take your analysis a step further by paying attention to how you spend your time *when you are most in control of it.* In other words, you can look at your free time. When we look at how we *choose* to spend our time, we can see how aligned our choices are with our hopes and dreams. This can be especially insightful for those of us who don't have as much leeway as we'd like when it comes to that work/school/childcare chunk of time.

When you remove work (or school or childcare) from your top activities, what do you see?

ACTUAL VS. DESIRED TIME SPENT

Now that you have a better picture of how you're spending your time, do you like what you see? Notice whether you are spending time on the things that bring you meaning and joy or those that push you away from your goals. Are you on track, spending time in support of your goals? Or might things need a little tweaking? You might find that you are on the right track but could make some small improvements. You might discover that things are completely out of balance and need to be right-sized. You may or may not feel that drastic changes are necessary. You might even be surprised by how you do spend your time. Sometimes, how we *think* we behave doesn't match up with our *actual* behavior.

WHERE DOES THE TIME GO?

PERCEPTION	REALITY
WORK	MEMES
SLEEP	DOOM-SCROLLING
CHORES	LIST MAKING
SOCIALIZING	TEXTING

For each item on your list, notice whether your *actual* time spent for each activity coincides with your *desired* time spent for each. Next to each item, put a small zero (0) for zero change, a plus sign (+) for more time desired, or a minus sign (-) for less time. If you are more or less happy with how you spend your time, great! If there's a gap, that's okay. There are likely many reasons for this disconnect: responsibilities, emotions, talents and skills, habits, and more. It's useful to see how the puzzle pieces are coming together and whether or not you like what you see. At this point, we're not committing to making changes yet; we are just getting a sense of what we're working with. In Part 3, we'll make an action plan for any necessary changes.

Ask yourself these questions:

- Am I happy with how I spend my time? Why or why not?

- Am I spending my time on the right things? To what degree?

- What's one small thing I can do today to shift my attention and spend my time more in line with my values, hopes, and dreams? (For example, you might cancel your Apple TV subscription or delete Instagram from your phone if you're spending too much time on these platforms.)

Five People

By now, you've charted your values and aspirations, and you have a snapshot of whether or not your daily activities are aligned with those goals. Now it's time to assess whether the company you keep can help you reach your goals, uphold your values, and encourage you to pursue those dreams and ambitions. In this section, we'll look at who you spend your time with and help you identify your biggest supporters as well as your detractors. The people we surround ourselves with matter more than we might think.

THE COMPANY YOU KEEP

According to many motivational speakers and entrepreneurs, our success is determined by the five people with whom we spend the most time. The idea is that people rub off on us; their ambitions, their work ethic, their worldview, and their hustle can all affect our own. As a result, some entrepreneurs ruthlessly pare down their friend group and network to only their most successful peers as if preparing for success by osmosis. If we are porous individuals, influenced by those around us, we might as well stack the deck in our favor, so the thinking goes. (This also explains why some parents favor certain friends for their children over others.) Success—be it in the form of money, fame, accolades, or college degrees—depends at least in part on who we spend our time with.

And yet, it's good to surround yourself with people who have different ambitions, work styles, backgrounds, and worldviews. Having people in our lives who will challenge our assumptions helps us see problems differently and can stoke our creativity in new ways, which can *also* help us reach our goals.

Who's in Your Corner?

Make a list of the five people you spend most of your time with on a daily basis. These may be physical or virtual connections. It's important that these five be a part of your every day since, as author Annie Dillard says, "How we spend our days is, of course, how we spend our lives." Be sure to write down who you are *actually* spending your time with—not who you *aspire* to spend your time with.

For many of us, groups like family, roommates, or coworkers will show up. Try to name specific individuals for the most accurate picture of who, exactly, you are most frequently in conversation with.

When you've finished, take a step back to reflect: What do you think about your list? Are you surprised by what you found? Upset by it? Ready to give yourself a pat on the back? Notice how you feel in response to what you've written. If you're like me, you might find that you spend a lot of time with people who it's *easy* to spend a lot of time with—which may not be in your best interest.

Promoters, Passives, and Detractors

Some of the people on our list will make us happy; we will be glad to see their names and think fondly of how they have supported, inspired, motivated, or simply understood us in the past. Others may be benign, neither inspiring nor dulling. But some may deflate our sense of self, cause us undue stress, undermine our efforts and ambitions, or even disrespect our ideals and values. Read these descriptions and consider who in your life fits into each bucket.

- **Promoters:** Promoters are all in on *you*. They believe in you and what you are capable of, and spread the word to others without being asked. They respect your work and are not competitive with it. If you're self-employed, promoters will send you referrals because they believe in you and your work. If you're working a nine to five, these are the former coworkers who will recruit you to their new employer. They want you around and aren't afraid to say it. They want to be on *your* top-five list!

- **Passives:** Many people in our life likely fit into this category: neither bringing you down nor elevating you to higher levels. They aren't trying to undermine you, but they're not boosting you up either. They may be perfectly pleasant company, without being a propeller or collaborator for your endeavors.

- **Detractors:** Beware of the detractors in your life. This group is more than likely to pull you down. They may sabotage your efforts with put-downs or passive-aggressive comments. They may gossip or bad-mouth you and your work. They may dominate your time such that you can't focus on your big hopes and dreams, or actively discourage you from pursuing your goals.

Taking a look at your list, place a small *PR*, *P*, or *D* next to each person's name. What do you think about what you see? For now, simply notice without judgment how your list is shaping up.

Net Promoter Scores

Promoters, passives, and detractors are terms used in Net Promoter Scores, or NPS. NPS is a popular tool in market research to learn about a customer's experience with a product, service, or brand. If you have ever taken a survey that has asked you how likely you are to recommend something to a friend on a scale of 0 to 10, you have encountered an NPS survey. We can use this rubric as inspiration for exploring how likely the main players in our lives are to support us in reaching our goals.

THE COMPANY YOU NEED

To truly live a purposeful and meaningful life, we might find that some adjustments are needed to our network of friends and colleagues. We need to ask ourselves: Do we have the right people on our personal team to help us realize our goals, aspirations, and intentions?

Now, I'm not talking about *help* in terms of having someone in your network who can introduce you to someone who might offer you your next job. These relationships, while incredibly useful, can quickly become transactional. I'm also not talking strictly about promoters who will sing our praises when we've reached a high point; they are wonderful, but we need other help along the way. We need the cheerleaders, advisors, and collaborators who are right there with us in the trenches of making or trying something new. Their help takes a different form: They may offer emotional support, creative thinking, or even life experience. I call them *gems*.

Gems

Gems are those people in our lives who help us feel our best. They accept us and recognize our talents and encourage us to go after what we want. They believe in our abilities and cheer us on when we experience self-doubt. They are honest with us when our behaviors are not in line with our values or when our skills and talents need honing. They bring levity when we are feeling discouraged, provide inspiration when we feel stuck, and take our ideas and feelings seriously when we are too afraid to. These people don't need business degrees or a high net worth to be valuable partners in life.

GEMS

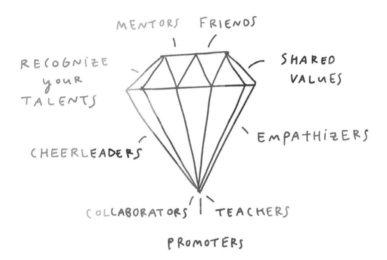

MENTORS FRIENDS
RECOGNIZE your TALENTS
SHARED VALUES
CHEERLEADERS
EMPATHIZERS
COLLABORATORS TEACHERS
PROMOTERS

Here are traits you might recognize in the gems in your life:

- Inspiring

- Motivating

- Challenge your ideas

- Help you get unstuck

- Sounding boards

- Advice givers

- Thoughtful peers and friends
- Equal parts role model, mentor, therapist, coach, co-conspirator in creative endeavors
- Energizers

Can you think of a gem in your life?

SELF-REFLECT

Where Are Your Gems?

As you take a look at the top-five list of people you spend most of your time with on a daily basis, mark a G next to your gems. How many gems are in your top five? Don't be alarmed if this number is smaller than you'd like it to be. It's not how many gems we have but how often we share moments with them that matters most.

Make a separate list for the gems in your life who aren't in your top-five list. This list can be as long or short as you'd like. Next to each name, write down one or two words that describe what you appreciate about them. This is not only a lovely exercise in gratitude (you can share those one or two words with these gems and thank them!) but also a way to discover or remind yourself of the qualities, traits, and values you admire in others as you grow your circle of gems, supporters, and promoters.

Whatever your final count of gems, let this be a gentle reminder to reach out more often—to not wait until they reach out to you or to worry if you seem overeager, but to simply create more moments of connection (in person, over the phone, or even online) with these very important people in our lives.

ACTUAL VS. DESIRED COMPANY

For various reasons—life circumstances, job, geography, and more—many of us will notice a gap between who we want to spend our time with and with whom we actually surround ourselves. When I ran my first life audit, some of the most inspiring people I know barely made it into the top ten people I interact with; I suspect this is true for many of us. Some of that will be out of our control—our gems may be in high demand and may not have as much time for us as we'd like. But some circumstances are within our control—perhaps *we* are the unavailable ones. Without blaming ourselves or others for any imbalance, it's useful to see where there is misalignment.

INSPIRING   AVAILABLE

↑
the SWEET
SPot

Identifying who is in our corner—and who is not (yet!)—can help us see where change might be needed. This doesn't have to be cutthroat; you do not have to upend your entire social circle or friend group (unless you want to). This is simply about being more aware of who you spend your time with and whether or not they are helping your cause—not just in terms of tangible advice, money, or skills but also with respect to emotional support, curiosity, and creative thinking. Knowing where you stand today can be a helpful start to getting to where you want to go.

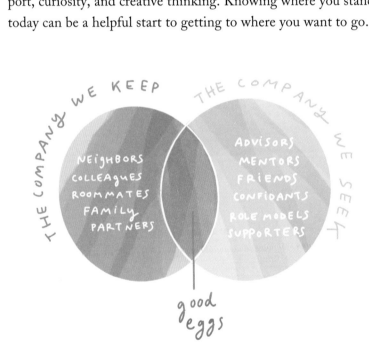

THE COMPANY WE KEEP

THE COMPANY WE SEEK

NEiGHBORS
COLLEAgUES
ROOMMATES
FAMILY
PARTNERS

ADVISORS
MENTORS
FRIENDS
CONFIDANTS
ROLE MODELS
SUPPORTERS

good eggs

Are You Happy with the Company You Keep?

SELF-REFLECT

Returning to your top-five people and gems lists, reflect on the following:

1. Who would you like to spend more time with? Put a small plus sign next to their names.

2. Spend less time with? Put a small minus sign there. (For example, perhaps you value honesty but have a particular friend who brings out the gossip in you.)

3. Whose company is just right? Add a checkmark.

4. Who do you need to reconnect with? Make a new list if needed.

Reflecting on your list, consider whether you are in good company for reaching your goals and living out your core values. If you are not happy with your list, what's getting in the way of spending time with the people you love and admire most? How might you connect with them more often and move them up on the ladder to your top five?

By now, you likely have some ideas about changes you'd like to make, even if you don't yet know how or when. Like Goldilocks, you might need to experiment to find the "just right" balance. In the next section, we'll get into the nitty-gritty of how to turn your life audit from insight into action and impact.

PART 2

UNDERSTAND YOUR LIFE AUDIT

Uncover Personal Insights

The Story of You • Perish or Nourish

Now that you have completed your life audit, it's time to make sense of it. You have all the raw data you need—on the pages of your notebook, in piles of sticky notes, and deep in your heart. Now it's time to turn this information into insight, numbers into narrative. In this section, you'll learn how to interpret your personal life audit. What do your sticky notes tell you about your life? What do your wishes say about you? In the pages to come, you'll uncover personal insights about you and your life audit.

The Story of You

In Part 1 we saw the breadth of our desires and mapped them into specific groupings. We got a snapshot of the areas we are most interested in pursuing, based on the quantity of wishes. We also discovered what our values are and how these are sometimes embedded in our goals. Now it's time to look at the whole picture. In this section, we want to go deeper. What can our themes collectively tell us about ourselves? This section will help you understand yourself better. We're going to tell the story of *you*.

KNOWN DESIRES

Your life audit results are a map of your desires. It shows you where you long for more, what is missing or absent in your life, and where there is potential for something new or different. Your life audit represents yearning but also opportunity. In this section, we will look at what you seek.

Sometimes our desires are obvious to us. We've wanted to take over the corporate world for as long as we can remember, or to have kids, or both. We've wanted to open a wine bar since the day we turned twenty-one or be a competitive swimmer since our first time in the pool. We've always been creative, or good with numbers, or family-oriented, or a loyal friend. We've long had a passion for fashion or a flair for home decor. We've always loved the movies. So when we see wishes like "Open a wine bar," or "Make time for my friends," or "Redo my wardrobe," or "Get that promotion," we aren't surprised. These desires make us think, "That sounds like me," or "That sounds right." It can be comforting to see ourselves so clearly in our goals.

In my first life audit, one of my biggest piles was a category I called *skills* for the many skills I wanted to acquire. I wasn't surprised to see it on paper because I know I am happiest when I'm learning. Chasing learning curves has always been a priority for me. It made me happy to see this theme so prominently featured—it felt aligned with who I was, what I valued, and what I believed in. It was, in a word, so *me*.

As you reflect on your ranked list of themes, ask yourself:

- **What feels familiar, known, or unsurprising to me?**

- **Why do these wishes feel familiar?** (For example, they might be reflections of ongoing interests, passions, or even preoccupations and challenges.)

- **What is motivating these familiar desires? Why do I still want to achieve these goals?**

- **How do I feel about seeing these familiar wishes?**

HIDDEN DESIRES

Sometimes our desires will be obvious to us, but sometimes they are buried beneath the surface, emerging only when we are honest with ourselves and give ourselves the time and space to understand them. Even those of us who tend to be in tune with our wants and desires will likely discover something new about ourselves during our life audit. You might find that you've buried a wish so deep that you had no idea it existed. You may be surprised at something that feels out of character or simply doesn't align with how you see yourself. Each wish offers a moment of self-discovery.

In my most recent life audit, I found a number of wishes I grouped under the header of "personal reboot." Unlike previous life audits, this was the first time I had any wishes around revamping my look (hair, wardrobe, etc.). Before my life audit, these were fleeting thoughts that I paid little attention to. But seeing them all together, it dawned on me that these wishes were all signs that I was looking for a change—a physical transformation, an aesthetic refresh, something new and different from the usual. I'm guessing it's because I'm approaching my fortieth birthday—silly but true. Now I could see what it was I really wanted out of them.

Take a deep dive into your own desires now. Consider them for a moment, then answer the following questions:

- What feels new to me?

- What surprises me? What's unlike me in some way?

- What is motivating these new desires? Why do I want to reach these new goals?

- Which desires have I shared with others? Said out loud?

- Which desires have I kept a secret from myself or others? Why might that be?

HOW DO I FEEL ABOUT MY DESIRES?

While uncovering your desires, you've also likely felt a number of feelings and emotions in response to them—from wonder and surprise to familiarity and comfort, to excitement or trepidation. Now is the time to explore these feelings.

Inviting vs. Intimidating Activities

It took me many, many years to finally get my act together and produce a podcast, but seeing that goal appear so many years in a row during my annual life audit ritual eventually made it clear that this was not a passing interest and that I would need to prioritize it. Every additional year that I allowed myself to be daunted by the process, my life audit would serve as a reminder that I wasn't following through.

I AM UNEARTHING MY TRUE DESIRES

WHAT AM I AFRAID OF?

Of course, timing is everything, so that's not to say you must tackle everything in your life audit right away. (We'll talk about how to know when it's time to prioritize your goals in Part 3.) But it is important to tune into what feels inviting and what feels intimidating and to try to understand why.

Some of your wishes will feel immediately within reach. For others, you may need a pep talk to get started. If you find you are continually procrastinating on a given goal or are struggling to even get started, there is personal insight there. What might your slow starts and quick starts tell you about yourself?

Although we won't commit to specific wishes until Part 3, take a moment to briefly check in with yourself about where you feel inspired and encouraged and where you feel overwhelmed and intimidated. Your feelings can tell you something about what you believe is possible and what you believe you are capable of. They may be a sign of a mental or emotional block that needs addressing to see your dreams through. (We'll talk about the practical hurdles that may be in your way in Part 3.)

Consider the following questions:

- **Which activities in my life audit feel daunting?**

- **Why these?** (Notice any patterns as to which activities feel most intimidating, such as activities that require

trying something new, goals that are too large, or wishes
that are really obligations in disguise.)

- **How might I make things more inviting and less
  intimidating?**

- **Which wishes feel inviting?**

- **Why might that be?**

- **What might this tell me about what's working
  in this area?**

Deep-Seated Emotions

Your wishes might elicit specific emotional responses from you.
But it's also true that some of your wishes might even *stem from*
a particular feeling or emotion—although this isn't always obvious at first. For example, in my most recent life audit, I found
many desires around community, friendship, and relationships—
more so than any other year of conducting my annual life audit.
I thought about why this might be. After two years of braving
pandemic isolation, I had moved back to my hometown in
search of community. I was in a particularly open-minded phase
of my life, eager to expand my friendship circle and meet new
people. If I went a little deeper than that, I could admit this
wasn't entirely opportunistic. The truth is, I was lonely. It was
useful to understand that *loneliness* was what was motivating me.
It was a feeling I'd previously danced around and only admitted

to myself thanks to the necessary introspection of a life audit. It was clarifying to have a name for this feeling, and made it easier to think of ways to address it.

Ask yourself:

- **Which wishes stem from my emotions?**

- **Which emotions are they rooted in?**

- **What do my wishes tell me about how I have been feeling lately?**

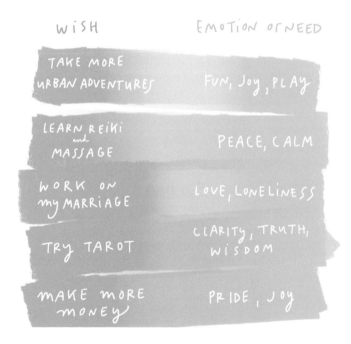

WISH	EMOTION or NEED
TAKE MORE URBAN ADVENTURES	FUN, JOY, PLAY
LEARN REIKI and MASSAGE	PEACE, CALM
WORK ON my MARRIAGE	LOVE, LONELINESS
TRY TAROT	CLARITY, TRUTH, WISDOM
MAKE MORE MONEY	PRIDE, JOY

WHAT DOES MY LIFE AUDIT SAY ABOUT ME?

If you've ever had a natal chart reading by an astrologer (or a life path reading by a numerologist, or used a Sorting Hat, taken a Myers-Briggs quiz or an Enneagram test, or another kind of typology or corporate astrology), you have probably heard things like "You're the type of person who . . ." "You're really good at . . ." or "You're naturally curious about . . ." But rather than look outward and have other people or programs tell you who you are, you can look inward instead. Your life audit is not only a reflection of your current wants and needs and values but also a detailed picture of who you are today.

You can discover this for yourself with a little introspection. Take a moment to review your themes and wishes from Part 1. Then reflect on the following questions:

- **What does your life audit tell you about your values and beliefs?**

- **What does it tell you about your ambitions?**

- **What does it tell you about your relationships?**

- **What does it tell you about your health?**

- **What does it tell you about your relationship with money?**

- **What does it tell you about your current mindset?**

- **What else do you notice?**

Reflecting on your list, you might see signs of your competitive nature, your ambitious personality, or your homebody tendencies. You might see your spending or planning tendencies come through. You might notice a newfound appreciation for beauty, art, luxury, and the finer things in life thanks to a new promotion. Or perhaps your life audit shows that your fighting temperament or conflict avoidance means that your relationships need work. Maybe your life audit is filled with signs that you want to be known in your industry, or that it is more important to you to connect within your immediate local community.

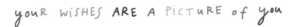

Whatever you notice, take heart in it—both the stuff that goes down easy and the stuff that's tougher to swallow. This is who you are today, every bit of it. How lovely!

In Part 3 we'll discuss tactical ways to double down on areas you are happy with and to make changes where you are not. You can shade your self-portrait in different colors or shapes if you have the right tools and know where to start.

KINDS OF ACTIVITIES

Anyone who knows me will not be surprised to hear that there aren't many sporty activities on my wish list. But there are always several creative categories, like writing, drawing, and podcasting. Seeing so many creative activities in my life audit year after year is reaffirming—it reminds me that I didn't just fall into my career as a writer and illustrator. I've gravitated toward it my whole life.

Take a moment to consider the following:

- **Which kinds of activities show up most frequently in your life audit?** (For example, are you drawn to taking classes? Learning things on your own? Doing group activities or solo ones?)

- **Are there overarching categories these activities fit into?** (For example, creative, athletic, cognitive, or spiritual, and so on. If your wishes are scattered across several areas, don't feel as if you need to wedge your activities into just one or two groups. Having a variety of activities that defy categorization is also a useful insight; it might indicate that you are more of a generalist than a specialist or that you have broad tastes and an open mind.)

Perish or Nourish

WHAT NEEDS
ATTENTION?

WHAT is WELL
TENDED?

As you look at your life audit, you will inevitably have opinions about the parts of your audit—and your life—you feel good about as well as those you feel disconnected from or are struggling to manage. There may also be wishes that are so new that you've yet to give them attention because they are so fresh. All is fair and normal!

In this section, we'll evaluate what needs attention, affection, or other resources like time and money to help you see your goals through. We'll also look at where you are already investing your time and resources, and make space to celebrate your efforts and progress.

WHAT NEEDS EXTRA ATTENTION?

Take a look at your life audit and make a list of the wishes that need attention from you in order for them to thrive. Although all of your goals, in theory, need your attention to be reached, some of them need a little bit extra. Start by noticing which goals and values have been neglected, deprioritized, ignored, or abandoned in the past. This is usually the case for repeat wishes—the wishes that appear in our New Year's resolutions, professional goal setting, and life audits year after year. Sometimes they reappear word for word ("quit my job"—for real this time!). Other times they take slightly different forms but remain more or less the same ("exercise more," "take a dance class," "get a gym membership," "improve my strength and flexibility," etc.). Repeat wishes often reappear with little or no progress. You might also need to dedicate extra attention to brand-new wishes that you are still trying to understand, or simply haven't had the time or energy to commit to yet. Ask yourself the following:

- **What needs extra attention from me?**

- **Where have I let my values lapse?**

- **Why might that be?**

Now, notice if there are any trends in what you find. For example, do you, like me, tend to deprioritize health goals? (Somehow these only seem to be a priority when I'm sick or injured or really feeling my age.) Or perhaps you've been wanting to learn a new language or skill for years, yet you still haven't booked a class. Ask yourself:

- **What kinds of values, goals, or wishes do you tend to kick-start?**

- **What kinds of values, goals, or wishes do you tend to struggle to see through?**

- **Why might that be?** (For example, you might find it difficult to complete goals that require collaboration, tend to be highly complex, stem from a particular feeling or emotion such as fear, or feel more like an obligation than a desire. Conversely, these things may be very motivating to you! It depends on the person.)

THERE

IS

SO MUCH

MORE

THAT I CAN

DO IN

THIS

WORLD

- What or who might be able to help?

- What is one small thing you can do today to nourish one of these wishes?

As you notice where your efforts have stalled out or suffered from a cold-start problem in the past, resist the urge to judge yourself. Instead, observe, reflect, and discover what needs tending with a spirit of curiosity and self-compassion. Give yourself an honest chance to learn what resources you might need to make progress in the future.

WHAT IS WELL TENDED?

While it's important to know what needs nourishment, it's also essential to recognize where we are already advancing our goals and living our values with ease. This is especially true given the very human tendency to focus on the negative (what we lack, where we may be falling short) rather than the positive (our achievements, efforts, commitment, and persistence). In this section, we will deliberately upend our negativity bias by making the space to recognize our efforts and unpack what's working, and when.

Taking a look at your life audit, make a list of the goals and values that have been well tended. These may be goals you are naturally drawn to or are simply "low-hanging fruit," easy to achieve because they are baked into your routine or job in some way. For example, if you love to write and also write for a living, it might be easier for you to dedicate your time to writing-centric goals than if you worked as an accountant. Other wishes, especially in the case of values or daily habits, may be so embedded into who you are that it would be harder to *not* live them than to see them through. Ask yourself:

- **Which goals, values, and wishes are well tended?**

- **Where have I upheld my values?**

- **Why might that be?**

As before, notice whether there are any trends in your list of well-nourished wishes and values. For example: Are you particularly effective at advancing professional goals? Do you excel at standing up for your beliefs even when it means taking an unpopular opinion? Are you an excellent steward of all things family-related?

Ask yourself:

- **What kinds of values, goals, or wishes do I regularly carry through?**

- **Why might that be?** (For example, perhaps they tend to be solo pursuits, have low complexity, or stem from a particular emotion, like joy.)

- **Who or what might have helped me nourish these wishes and goals?**

LOOK FOR SIGNS OF HIDDEN NOURISHMENT

Sometimes what we nourish is not specifically captured in our life audit. These might be areas of our life that are meaningful to us but appear surprisingly infrequently in our life audit, or not at all. They may be noticeably missing from your life audit, but there is a good reason for this.

For example, when I first ran my life audit, I was surprised to see that my family and adventure themes tallied low, despite how important they both are to me. Yet it was precisely because they are so central to my interests that they didn't show up as a goal or wish. I was already in the habit of prioritizing travel and family time. I didn't need to add a sticky note to wish for them: They were already ingrained in how I think about the future and how I live my day-to-day life. My low family and adventure rankings were actually signs of nourishment.

You can look for signs of hidden nourishment with a little self-reflection. Take a look at the major themes of your life audit and answer the following questions:

- **Which wishes look sparse at first glance but are actually well supported?**

- **What wishes are missing from your life audit because they are already well tended?**

- **Who or what is helping you cultivate these goals and wishes?**

- **How do you feel about these hidden pockets of progress?**

INGREDIENTS FOR SUCCESS

Often, it's when things are working well that we least interrogate them. The days that are smooth sailing, the moments we feel connected to our best selves, the projects we pursue that feel in line with our values—many of us prefer to enjoy the ride rather than ask ourselves why things are working well. This is a lovely approach; it allows us to live in the moment and savor it. But it's also useful to know why those days, moments, and projects are working so well. Working backward and piecing together what makes them so powerfully aligned to our wishes can be enlightening.

When you find something well-tended, you may decide to maintain your current approach, lean into it and accelerate your progress, switch things up for an improved outcome, or simply relish it. You might even express gratitude and share a thank you with someone in your life—including yourself.

Take a moment to reflect on your efforts:

- **In areas that are well tended, which skills, talents, or strategies have helped you to uphold these values and make progress on these wishes in the past?**

- **Whose support was valuable?**

- **What *kind* of support was most useful?** (For example, advice, cheerleading, permission to take breaks, caretaking, life admin help, etc.)

HONOR WHAT'S WORKING

Take a moment to appreciate all that you've done and continue to do in these areas. Some of us will find this natural (pat on the back for me!). Some of us may have become accustomed to trivializing our efforts and find it uncomfortable or silly to focus on what's working well. But recognizing our talents and efforts is important.

Each success holds a history of hard work, sacrifice, and deliberation within it. Your skills, your talents, your critical thinking have all played a role in getting to where you are. This is worth paying attention to. Knowing what's working well means you can replicate these efforts for future goals. You don't have to reinvent the wheel when you already know what you're good at. You can move more strategically and efficiently when you know how to work with what you've got.

Reflecting on what's working well also reminds us that we are capable. We have done great things before, and we can do it again. We have already set the foundation for what we want to do next. In joyful celebration, we gain momentum for pursuing bigger, more daring dreams in the future.

Now is a great time to stretch your body, roll out your neck, and shake your hands out before moving to the next section.

PART 3

CHART A PATH FORWARD

Put Your Life Audit into Action

Plot Your Wishes by Time • Prioritize • Make an Action Plan • Commit • Identify Roadblocks and Hurdles • Resources to Stay on Track • Stay Motivated

In this section, we move from insights to action. We'll look at actionable ways to break new ground and to make early progress in areas that are not yet well tended, as well as accelerating your progress where heat already exists. We'll determine which goals to pursue and when and make sure that you have the right people, strategies, and tools to turn your life audit dreams into reality. It's time to do something about all those beautiful dreams.

Plot Your Wishes by Time

The first time I conducted my life audit, I remember looking at my wish list with a mix of excitement and trepidation. I had a clear view of what was important to me, and there was a lot. Where to begin? To help prevent analysis paralysis, I decided to map my desires on a spectrum of "when." This would give me a sense of when to focus on which wishes. As I examined my life audit, three categories emerged:

1. **Always:** Core values and intentions to live by every day. One of mine is "To share what I've learned in life and professionally."

2. **Soon:** Wishes that were immediately actionable but in need of next steps and prioritization. In theory these could be undertaken in the next six to twelve months, such as my personal goal "To publish a podcast series."

3. **Someday:** Milestone moments and long-term goals; for instance, "To be spry at eighty."

No matter how many wishes you come up with, you might look at your map of goals and interests and think, "Amazing!" but also "Oh boy!" In this section, we'll use *time* as our primary dimension to map our goals and desires. This is the first step to making them more manageable and actionable.

ALWAYS (CORE VALUES AND INTENTIONS)

Always wishes are those we carry with us day-to-day, such as "to be more generous" or "to be a good friend." How do your values show up in your life audit results? Looking at your wishes, draw a heart on any sticky notes that reflect a mantra, core value, or intention you wish to live by every day.

SOON (NEAR-TERM GOALS)

Soon goals are those you'd like to tackle sooner rather than later, with *soon* meaning "in the next six to twelve months." Often, it's the culmination of our near-term goals (learn ProTools) and our core values (persistence) that lead us to eventually completing our *someday* goals (produce a podcast).

Soon goals might look like:

- Get off my family cell plan
- Take a rock climbing class
- Volunteer at the local soup kitchen
- Publish my first blog post
- Go on more date nights
- Get a personal trainer

Looking at your goals, draw an arrow on any sticky notes that reflect something you want to do in the near term.

SOMEDAY (LONG-TERM GOALS)

Someday goals are future aspirations. These are hopes and goals you have for yourself "at some point" in your life. Often, these goals serve as a North Star to help us organize our shorter-term goals into alignment.

Someday goals might look like:

- To make $100,000 by the time I am thirty

- To fall in love

- To open a café

- To start a business

- To learn a new language

- To host a podcast

- To buy a house

- To learn Reiki

- To publish a children's book

- To hit a bestseller list

Looking at your goals, draw a star on any sticky notes that reflect something you want to do someday in the future.

In some cases, you may feel that a wish could be a *soon* or a *someday*. Notice when you feel this tension and do your best to put a stake in the ground. We'll continue to refine this in the next section.

TALLY WISHES BY TIME

Note how many themes fit within each time frame. From this vantage point, you will see more clearly the wishes you could pursue now but have not yet prioritized, those you want to do at some point, and those you want to carry with you and live out each day. (You can see what mine looked like in my first audit on page 116.)

We'll look more deeply at how to best prioritize next.

Prioritize

Your life audit provides a detailed look at what you want to achieve in your lifetime, with a loose approximation of when you'll pursue which goals (*always*, *soon*, *someday*). But in order to move the ball forward, we need to get specific. We need to know exactly where to start. How many *soon* wishes will we take on this year? Which *someday* goals should we start chipping away at and which can wait? You may have lots of ideas and endless enthusiasm for getting started, or you may be feeling daunted by all that you want to achieve. Prioritization ensures that we don't overcommit and wear ourselves out before we've had a chance to get started. It keeps us optimistic *and* realistic. The following pages will help you prioritize which top five wishes to pursue from your life audit.

WAYS TO PRIORITIZE

As you may have noticed by now, there are many ways you can slice data to make sense of it. Each time we synthesize our wishes and discover new themes, we create a new narrative or way of understanding it. We write a new story for who we are, what we believe, and what we want out of this life.

Prioritization works similarly: You can prioritize your goals based on any number of criteria, each of which tells a different story about what is most important to you. There are many ways to make the case that *this* is the set of goals you'll pursue first. You have to find the method that feels right to you.

ASPIRATIONS   ON   A

FAMILY . . . .
COMMUNITY . . . .
ADVENTURE . . . .
FINANCIAL HEALTH . . . . . .
PHYSICAL HEALTH . . . .
MENTAL HEALTH . . . .
CREATIVE PROJECTS . . . . .
SKILLS . . . .
PROFESSIONAL . . . .
WRITING . . . .
DESIGN . . . .
GIVING BACK . . . .

SPECTRUM of WHEN

♥♥♥♥ ★ >

★★ >>>>

♥ ★★★★ >

★★★★★★★ >>

♥♥ ♥♥♥ ★★★ >>

♥♥♥♥♥♥♥♥ ♥♥♥♥ ★★ >>

♥ ★★★★ >>

★ ★★★★★★ >>>>>>

♥ ♥♥♥ ★★★★★ ★

★★★★★★ >>>>>

★★★★ >>>>>>

♥♥♥ ★★ >>

★ ♥ = alwAyS   ★ = SomEDAy   > = SOON

Here are a few ways you might consider prioritizing your wishes:

- **By emotion:** Choose what makes you scared, excited, joyful, or a mix.

- **Using rational thinking:** Start with what you know you can achieve and consider which resources you have in place or how reaching one goal will help you reach others.

- **By complexity:** Choose many small, straightforward goals you know you can easily achieve or select only a handful of stretch goals to work toward.

- **By resources:** Consider how "expensive" a goal will be to fulfill (in time, money, equipment, or other resources) or estimate how much time will be needed to complete it (due to its complexity or scope), versus which goals have little start-up cost.

- **By the numbers:** Use the frequency of how often a goal, value, or wish appears in your life audit and which themes are most numerous as your guides and go with your biggest piles first.

- **By intuition:** Go with your gut and trust it's telling you where to start for a reason.

Take a minute to reflect on how your top wishes might change depending on the framework you choose. This is an opportunity to see things from different perspectives, experiment with your vision of what's most important, question your assumptions, and explore. Here are some thought-starters to consider:

Emotion

- Which goals am I most afraid of? Most confident in?

- Which goals do I feel no emotional connection to at all? (This may be a sign that these are "shoulds" rather than true desires. Set these aside for now.)

- Tuning into my emotions, which wishes or goals would I choose for this year?

Rational thinking

- Which goals are most practical to pursue at this moment in time?

- Using rational thinking, which wishes or goals would I choose for this year?

Complexity

- Which goals are high effort? (These may include goals that require significant set-up or ramp-up time.)

PLOT WISHES

WARM
EMOTIONS
(PASSION,
EXCITEMENT,
CONTENTMENT)

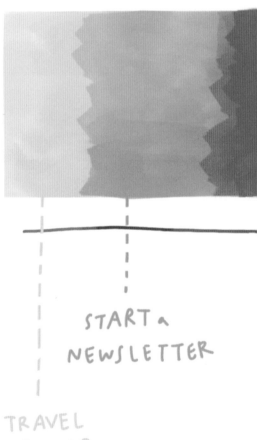

START a
NEWSLETTER

TRAVEL
ABROAD

BY EMOTION

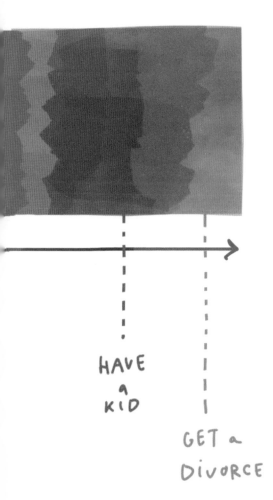

COOL
EMOTIONS
(FEAR, ANGER,
INSECURITY)

HAVE
a
KID

GET a
DiVORCE

- Which goals are low effort? (These may be easy to get started or see through.)

- Given their complexity, which wishes or goals would I choose for this year?

Resources

- Which goals require additional resources? (Resources might include time, money, equipment, or support from specific people, such as caregivers, experts, friends, and family.)

- Given the resources needed, which wishes or goals would I choose for this year?

Quantity

- Which high-level theme or grouping has the highest quantity of wishes? The lowest?

- Which wishes repeat themselves in different forms throughout my life audit? (For example, you might find that a handful of wishes really boil down to one.)

- Given their quantity, which wishes or goals would I choose for this year?

Intuition

- Which areas am I most naturally drawn to?

- Following my intuition, which wishes or goals would I choose for this year?

YOUR TOP FIVE

It's time to narrow down and finalize your selection. Which wishes feel most present to you now? Which feel most pressing to pursue? Choose your top *five* to pursue *this year*.

Why five? It's a simple way to avoid the stress of over-committing and improves your odds of getting some wins in. It allows you to pace yourself over the course of the next twelve months. It also leaves space for the possibility that your wishes may change in future years, over the course of your lifetime.

Five is, of course, a target number: Your mileage may vary. If you pick five "easy" wishes to fulfill, then adding a few stretch goals might make sense. If you pick five complex goals to achieve, you might consider paring those down to just two or three or changing the balance so that you have a variety of complex and readily achievable goals. Choosing a mix across *always*, *soon*, and *someday* goals is another way to find balance.

Some people may even find that picking five broad themes, rather than specific goals, is the best fit for them—if you like to have a North Star but don't want a step-by-step road map, that might work well for you.

Of course, if five intuitively feels like overkill, choose fewer! You can always go back and add more as you achieve your goals. My five will be different from your five no matter how we slice it—and that's a good thing.

To help you choose your top five goals or themes, ask yourself these questions:

- **Which goals and intentions are my highest priority?** (Choose whichever prioritization criteria feels right to you.)

- **What drew me to these wishes?** (Knowing your purpose can be especially grounding as you begin to pursue your goals.)

- **Which wishes do I actually have time for this year?** (Look for areas of potential overwhelm and consider whether you will change your top five or make other adjustments in your life to support them.)

Jot down your five winners on a sticky note. Consider putting the note where you'll regularly see it, such as a bathroom mirror, computer monitor, or journal, to remind you of what you've set out to achieve.

GUT CHECK

Now that you have your top five, stop and take a moment to look at them with a hopeful but critical eye. Ask yourself whether any changes are needed to set you up for success. If you're happy with your selection, move on to action planning. If not, take some time to make any necessary tweaks before you begin the next section. Ask yourself:

- Are my top five aspirations realistic?

- Am I biting off more than I can chew, or not enough?

- What needs to be deprioritized to set me up for success?

- Over what timeline can I reasonably accomplish these goals?

I WANT TO DO THE THINGS I'VE ALWAYS SAID I WANTED TO DO

Make an Action Plan

Now that you have your top five goals, you might feel pressured to check these items off your list as soon as possible. But remember, your timeline is your *entire life*, so there's no need to rush to do it all—it's a *life audit*, after all. It is good to make progress, but unnecessary and unproductive to tackle everything at once. Instead, we can be strategic about when to pursue what. What follows are a few ways to play the long game.

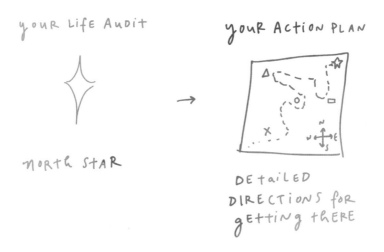

GIVE YOURSELF A YEAR

I generally recommend that you give yourself a grace period of a full year for achieving goals and fulfilling wishes. Why a year? It's enough time for you to pursue big fish and little fish. Some dreams are so big they may need to be broken up into smaller steps to complete. Others might require a certain level of physical fitness, emotional strength, or mental clarity to pursue—and you might not be feeling those things yet. A year gives you a chance to see meaningful changes. You will never regret giving yourself time to set yourself up for success and get it right.

Take a look at your top five wishes and consider the following:

- **Which goals or wishes might benefit from being pursued on a longer timeline?**

- **How do these goals fit alongside my other long-term priorities?**

- **Are any of my top five wishes *multiyear* projects?**

- **Do any of my top five goals require *less than a year* to complete?**

START DURING THE RIGHT SEASON

Having our top five wishes for the year is a great start, but we can also look at smaller units of time to guide us on our journey. Certain goals will benefit from being anchored to specific months, quarters, or seasons. There may also be external factors that are important to pay attention to, like when budgets are assigned or what busy and slow periods look like for your industry.

You might time your goals to take advantage of what behavioral economist Katy Milkman calls the "fresh-start effect"—moments in the calendar year (think back-to-school, the new year, or the first day of spring) that offer fresh starts and give us a better chance of forming new habits and seeing our goals through. Milestone moments of transition such as starting a new job, moving to a new city, or becoming a parent also count as fresh starts.

Or, you may simply be someone who benefits from structure and prefers a quarterly approach; committing to fulfilling one wish every two to three months might be best for you. It all depends on what you need to succeed as well as the size and complexity of a given wish or desire.

Answer the following questions with your top five wishes in mind:

- Which goals or wishes might benefit from being pursued over several months?

- Would any of my goals or wishes benefit from being pursued during a specific month or season?

- What responsibilities, industry trends, or obligations should I consider when mapping my wishes to seasons?

WEEKLY INTENTIONS

Many of us will find it difficult to commit to fulfilling one wish or goal per week, but we *can* break a larger wish down into its component parts and map *those* week over week. For example, if you wish to launch a podcast, you might take a moment to map each of the major steps or phases of production from week to week—from brainstorming and planning, to interviewing and hosting, to postproduction and editing, to marketing and publicity efforts. Although it is likely that weekly targets will change over time, given what you'll learn about the amount of time, effort, and resources involved at each step, having weekly targets can nonetheless help guide you toward progress.

Keeping your top five wishes in mind, consider the following thought-starters:

- **Which goals or wishes might benefit from being mapped out week over week?**

- **Which steps or phases could be completed on a weekly basis?**

- **Which responsibilities, industry trends, or obligations should I consider when mapping my wishes to weeks?**

Many of us will benefit from this kind of added structure, but if mapping things week over week feels contrary to how you see things through, feel free to skip this step.

DAILY INTENTIONS

The only wishes I recommend attempting to complete on a daily basis are values, or your *always* wishes. Our values shape who we are and how we move through the world day after day. They can be the inspiration for a wish or bring meaning to it. For example, one of the values that appeared in my most recent life audit is to foster my son's connection to his Latin American roots. This isn't something that will be done in a year, but something I'm committed to doing for the rest of my life. This value drives my behavior on everything from FaceTiming with the abuelos, to sending him to a Spanish immersion after school program, to planning future vacations to Argentina and Colombia (where my parents are from), to speaking to my son in Spanish (and committing to looking up the Spanish words when my vocabulary isn't adequate). I don't need to map this out on an annual or even weekly basis because it is already ingrained in me—it is a strong belief and value I hold dear that I try to live out with intention every day.

Similarly, you may not need reminders or action plans to live out your values every day. It may be intrinsic to you to experience more art and culture in your city, to express gratitude to those around you, to stay curious and pursue knowledge and new experiences wherever you go, to be a part of your local community, or to make your house a home. We all have values, intentions, and ideals that are a part of us, ready to be expressed.

Ask yourself the following:

- **Which values, ideals, and intentions am I already living on a daily basis?**

- **How does this make me feel?**

- **Which additional values, ideals, or intentions do I want to live out every day?**

- **What are some small ways I might do this?**

WHO DO I WANT IN MY CORNER?

Commit

Many plans are good in theory, but can easily fail if our commitment falters. Committing means telling ourselves, "This is worth doing, even if it gets difficult." It is a way of telling others, "I am going to try something, and I might need your help, encouragement, or support." Committing helps us to stay loyal to our desires and avoid making excuses or hiding behind other responsibilities when the going gets tough. It is a way to be true to ourselves—to honor what we want and give ourselves the gift of seeing it through. Here are a few tools to help you commit to your life audit action plan.

ACCOUNTABILITY CIRCLES

When we embark on something new, it can be tempting to keep it a secret; if we fail, no one has to know. Yet sharing our ambitions with others can make our pursuits more tangible and successful. Sometimes we need to be accountable—not just to ourselves, but to others—to make things stick.

Accountability circles are groups of people who can help keep you on track. Circles can be formal, like joining a writing group that meets once a month and exchanges pages for feedback, having a business partner or collaborator with whom you regularly meet up to share progress, or starting a peer-coaching group with like-minded friends or colleagues.

Accountability circles can also be informal, such as a loose set of people who will champion your progress, help you think through roadblocks, ask questions to encourage you to try something different when you're stuck, or share their expertise, advice, and mentorship in the area you wish to pursue. Because you have engaged with them, they become invested in your progress. They may want to know whether you followed their advice and if it was helpful, or they may simply want to see you happy because they know how important this goal is to you. Some members of your accountability circle may be gems you know well, while others may be experts in your field or people you have hired to help you reach a large goal. Your circle could even be an online community of strangers who are pursuing a similar goal. Accountability circles can be composed of friends, family, acquaintances, or professionals.

My accountability circle includes people who love to hear updates on my latest creative projects and get joy from my pursuits, like my family and close friends; people whose interests are financially aligned with mine, such as my agent and my editor; and people who are tackling similar challenges, like fellow writers, authors, and creatives.

Take a moment to outline your ideal accountability circle. Get as specific as you can (take names!). List the people you want cheering you on, offering advice, or simply providing company on your journey.

LIFE AUDIT GROUPS

Life audit groups are a simple way to create a formal accountability circle around your goals. You can start your own life audit circle for mutual support and commitment among friends. These groups conduct their audits alone or silently side by side and link up afterward for shared accountability. Each person shares the top three areas they want to work on. In response, the group can offer advice, problem-solving, and encouragement. They can also help you stay on track and reinforce your goals, which can be as simple as asking, "How's your sleep going?" the next time you meet. Whether your fellow life auditors share similar wishes or wildly different ones, they can become trusted partners with whom you can both celebrate and commiserate on progress together. For more on group life audit sessions, see page 179. Consider the people in your life whom you can call, text, direct message, or email to share your goals with.

WHO DO YOU WANT

My IDEAL ACCOUNTABILITY CIRCLE

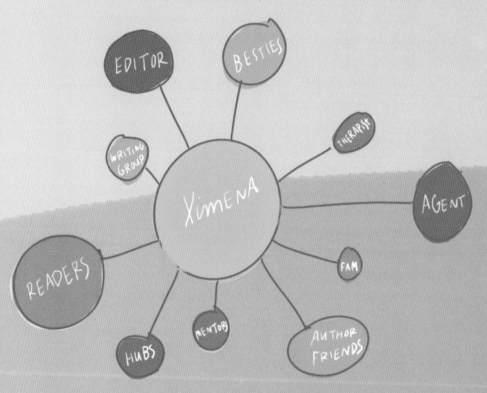

in your CORNER?

YOUR IDEAL ACCOUNTABILITY
CIRCLE

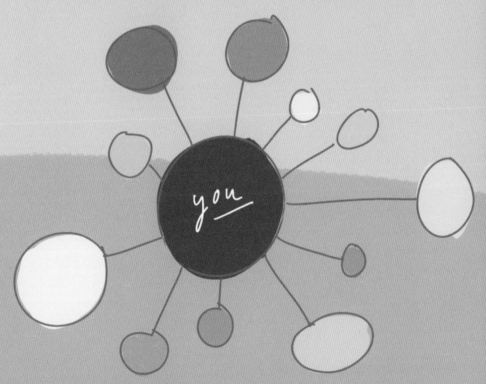

DEADLINES

Deadlines are not sexy, but they can help get you where you want to be. For each of your goals, figure out a rough estimate of how much time it will take to complete. Break up your primary deadline into a few smaller ones if the goal is particularly big or complex. This also gives you additional opportunities to celebrate—the more milestones you hit, the more occasions you have to pat yourself on the back and recognize your efforts and progress.

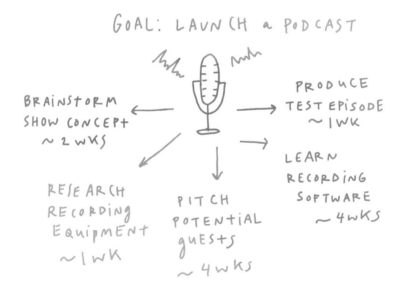

GOAL: LAUNCH a PODCAST

BRAINSTORM SHOW CONCEPT ~ 2 WKS

PRODUCE TEST EPISODE ~ 1 WK

RESEARCH RECORDING EQUIPMENT ~ 1 WK

PITCH POTENTIAL GUESTS ~ 4 WKS

LEARN RECORDING SOFTWARE ~ 4 WKS

As you think about your goals, ask yourself:

- **What deadlines can I commit to?**
- **How can I keep myself accountable to these deadlines?**
- **Are there other ways to show my commitment if I don't want to stick to a calendar deadline?** (For example, signing up for a yoga class with a friend to help you stick to a new exercise routine; announcing a project you plan to undertake in a blog post or newsletter to your network; proposing a new local composting program in an email to your neighborhood association, etc.)

Many of us dislike deadlines but ultimately find them useful motivators for getting things done. However, if you are the type of person who finds deadlines to be discouraging or stifling, you might find it best to skip this particular approach to accountability and try a different one.

SELF-CHECK-INS

Committing to your goals is ultimately an act of self-care, self-respect, and self-love. These are the wishes that we want to come true, the desires within us that deserve and need our nurturing. It is useful to check in with ourselves along the way—to reconnect with why we are doing this work, to remember what we are striving for, to discover whether these desires have changed or are still strong, and to recognize the benefits of our commitment. A self–check-in can be as informal or as ritualized as you want it to be. Your self–check-in might be a weekly journal entry, a walk in the park dedicated to reflecting on your desires and your progress, a few minutes during your commute home connecting with yourself and your wishes, or an occasional visit to a cozy coffee shop where you do little more than stare off into space, enjoy a pastry, and think about how you feel about your goals and how far you've come.

Here are some questions to consider as you check in with yourself:

- **Do I still feel connected to my desires? Do I need to let go of any wishes?**

- **Do I need to adjust my expectations of what I can accomplish this year, this month, or this week?**

- **Do I have the right people, tools, skills, and routines to help me make progress?**

- **Which personal qualities am I grateful to have with me on this journey?**

- **What progress and effort can I celebrate?**

Identify Roadblocks and Hurdles

There are many reasons why we might not see our dreams through—some tangible, some as shapeless as the wind. Perhaps you didn't know you had these dreams—that is what Part 1 was for. Perhaps you had not yet admitted—to yourself or others—how deeply you wanted these wishes to come true. Perhaps you had not yet committed to making them happen, as we did in Part 2. Perhaps there is something else making it difficult to realize our goals.

In every hero's journey, there are tests or challenges to face. It is normal to meet hurdles and setbacks, but we can prepare ourselves. If we can identify likely obstacles and anticipate common roadblocks, we can mitigate any damage or setbacks. When we know what's getting in our way, it's easier to overcome. When we don't know what's standing between us and our dreams, it can be difficult to make progress. We might pick the wrong battle, or make inconsequential changes when critical changes are needed. Now is the time to uncover our personal roadblocks and hurdles so that we can conquer them.

NOTES from the FIELD

Identifying Friction

In the field of user experience, or UX, *friction* refers to how easy or difficult it is to complete a given task. Friction can refer to anything from the number of steps required to complete a task (e.g., a lengthy registration process for a new service versus a short one) to how difficult they are to complete (e.g., having to fish out your ID to open an online bank account or navigating a help center that is only partially in your language). In some cases, friction can be good—when you are about to make a large purchase online, you might welcome the chance to confirm your purchase several times before it goes through to ensure you're spending the right amount. But usually, friction is frustrating, and it can deter us from completing our tasks or reaching our goals. In UX, this usually causes *drop-off*, meaning that an individual has dropped off, or given up on, the task at hand. If you've ever closed your laptop in frustration or said, "Forget it, I'll do this later" during a sign-up flow, you have dropped off. The same can happen in pursuit of our life audit goals. Friction can come in the form of a spouse, a child, or a pet who interrupts our focus; by our own self-interruptions, like checking email, news alerts, and social media; by a lack of expertise, skill, or understanding; or even come in the form of dreary weather, which can make it hard for many of us to get started. To beat friction, you have to know what's causing it.

WHAT'S STANDING IN YOUR WAY?

Any artist knows that having built-in constraints, such as the size of a canvas, a faulty camera, or a beautiful fabric available in only one color, can lead to creative problem-solving and unexpected, innovative results. But other constraints can be less useful, such as limits placed on our abilities either by ourselves or others, or even society at large.

WHAT'S STANDING IN YOUR WAY?

SELf-Limiting BELIEfs   PARENTAL PRESSURE   SOCIETAL EXPECTATIONS

No matter who we are, we all face limitations in our lives. There are four kinds of roadblocks that crop up most often. Here are some examples of the hurdles you might face in pursuit of your dreams:

- Responsibilities

- Resources

- Skills

- Feelings and emotions

To help you determine your *personal* roadblocks, we'll look at each of these categories in the following pages. Knowing which kinds of hurdles we most frequently face can help us learn how to surmount them.

Responsibilities

Existing responsibilities are often the biggest blocker to fulfilling new goals. As you might have discovered from your five activities list in Part 1, the bulk of our time goes to one of three places: jobs, schooling, or children. Our free time tends to be split between meaningful activities (such as catching up with old friends), necessary obligations (including life administration, caring for our homes, grocery shopping, and so on), and meaningless time sucks (like doomscrolling). As you commit to new goals, you'll likely have to drop something from your list of commitments. (Or cut into your sleep, which I don't recommend.) Your new goals will likely compete against your current responsibilities. Ask yourself these questions:

- Which responsibilities and obligations do I anticipate getting in the way of my goals?

- What is the nature of these responsibilities? (For example, they may be social, academic, professional, or familial.)

Many of us think of our responsibilities as fixed in place—necessary obligations with no wiggle room to them. But what if we could flex those responsibilities? Even the busiest of us often have a little more flexibility than we think. As you assess your situation, ask yourself:

- Which of my responsibilities and obligations are real versus perceived? (A *real* obligation includes things you are contractually bound to do, such as completing a project you are hired for. A *perceived* obligation might feel indisputable but is actually a fungible belief or expectation. For example, you might do the laundry for your family because of an unspoken assumption about whose responsibility it is to keep clothes and linens clean, not because others in your household are incapable of doing it.)

- When do these responsibilities increase? Are there busy periods I need to work around? (For example, if you are the primary cook in your household, you might find that the holidays are more intense than quiet months like February or October.)

- **When do these responsibilities decrease? Are there slow periods I can take advantage of?**

- **What kind of influence or agency can I exert over my responsibilities?** (These actions can be big, like quitting a job, or small, such as taking a real lunch break instead of working and eating at your desk.)

- **Who can I ask for help to relieve some of these responsibilities?** (This person might be in your home, network, school, organization, city council, or even the federal government.)

- **Which responsibilities and obligations can be adjusted so I can reach my goals?**

Resources

There are many resources that can make it easier for you to reach your goals and make your wishes come true. Not having the right resources in place can make it harder. Here are some resources that can affect your ability to fulfill your desires:

- Equipment

- Space

- Time

- Money

- Legal and administrative support

If you are missing crucial resources needed to see your goals through, see if there are small ways to access them. For instance, perhaps you can't purchase a fancy camera for a photography class, but you might be able to rent one or borrow one from the library. You might also consider a barter or swap with someone from your accountability circle or network. If you need peace and quiet to write your dream novel but can't concentrate with your adorable but noisy young children at home, you might offer to pet sit or water your single friend's plants while they're out of town and snag some quiet solo time for a few days. If you've done a group life audit session, see whether there are others in the group who can offer resources you don't have, and do the same for them. You might be surprised to learn who is great at reading contracts as well as who needs help with something you're good at.

What Resources Do You Need?

Think about the resources you have at your disposal today to make your life audit dreams come true, and which you could use more of. Grab a pen and paper and draw a chart with three columns to answer the following questions:

1. Which resources do you feel are missing from your toolkit? Make a list of anything that comes to mind. Put these in the first column.

2. Why might that be? For each resource, put your answer for why it may be missing in the next column.

3. Who or what could help? (For example, think about who you can call for a favor or what you can borrow from a public institution.) Put these in the third column.

4. What is one small step you can put into action today to access this resource? Write this down for later, or stop now to put wheels in motion on this small step.

Skills

Some goals require more effort than others. Fulfilling a high-level goal of bringing more art and culture into your life may be easier than becoming fluent in German. Where the former might mean getting a library card, becoming a member of your local museum, or going to more performances or concerts, the latter might mean signing up for a language class, finding a

German-speaking community, hiring a tutor, studying abroad, or even relocating abroad to reach your goal. In some cases, we will need to acquire new skills or improve existing ones in order to fulfill our deepest desires. These skills might be cognitive, emotional, physical, linguistic, technological, or creative, depending on the project you're pursuing.

Ask yourself:

- What new skills do I anticipate needing to reach my goal?

- Which skills that I already have need improving?

- Where might I learn these new skills or refine the ones I have?

- Who can teach me?

- Are there other ways I can access these skills? (For example, hiring an expert.)

- How long will I need to learn or refine these skills?

It is possible that you will not be interested in learning certain skills but find that they are necessary to reach your goal. (For instance, you might have zero interest in learning audio editing software but need it if your goal is to host a podcast.) But you also might discover subjects you didn't know you'd love or excel in. (Who knew you were great at drawing?) You might even get to flex skills that you're already great at, like master planning, hosting, or communicating. Open yourself to learning and improving no matter where you are in life or your level of skill. If it supports your goals, it's worth exploring.

Feelings and Emotions

Our feelings and emotions can encourage us to pursue our goals, but they can also sometimes get in our way. Consider whether any of the following feelings or emotions play a role in the story you tell yourself about your dreams:

- Fear
- Shame
- Guilt
- Passion
- Joy
- Curiosity
- Self-doubt
- Courage

- People-pleasing
- Imposter syndrome
- Feeling like an outsider
- Peer pressure
- Embarrassment
- Anxiety
- Depression
- Wonder

It's normal to experience any and all of these emotions. The key is to figure out what to do with them. Will your negative emotions grind your progress to a halt, or will you see them, accept them, and move forward anyway? Can you find a way to spin them on their head and use them for motivation? Consider the following questions as you reflect on your goals:

- Which goals and wishes am I proud to see in my life audit?

- Which goals or wishes do I feel squeamish about? Embarrassed by? Ashamed of? Sad about? Discouraged by?

- Can I flip or reframe any discouraging feelings into encouragement?

- Which encouraging feelings come up for me? What energizes and excites me? What makes me smile?

- Can I channel these feelings to get myself started? How might I reconnect with them when I hit a stumbling block?

- Would it help to speak with a confidante, therapist, coach, or someone else to process any of these feelings and emotions?

WHICH

WISHES

REQUIRE

BRAVERY?

External Influences

Sometimes we are the source of our personal challenges; at other times we are deeply influenced by the voices around us. (For most of us, it's a mix of the two.) Just as it is useful to know when we are getting in our own way, it also helps to notice when others are actively bringing us down or inadvertently challenging our ability to see things through. These negative influences might include the following:

- Partners
- Friends
- Children
- Employers
- Cultural and societal expectations

These forces and voices can be at odds with our innermost desires. For example, if you are a mother, it might be hard to take that weekend pottery workshop if you believe the societal message that your children come above all else, including your own happiness and relaxation. If you have a boss who works long hours and expects you to do the same, it might be difficult to fully unplug and reach for your journal at the end of a long day.

We may also find that we need words of encouragement for particularly daunting goals. If our partner expresses little interest when we share a fragile but important dream, we can feel deflated by their disinterested response. Sometimes, the very fact that they are *not* encouraging us to explore new territory or break new creative ground can be enough to stop us in our tracks.

As you think about your external influences, consider the following:

- **Which voices feel most present and influential in my life today?** (These can be specific individuals or broader cultural forces.)

- **Which voices have discouraged me from pursuing my dreams in the past?**

- **Whose voices have encouraged me?**

- **Whose voices do I want to amplify?**

- **Whose voices would I prefer to hear less loudly?**

If someone's voice is getting in the way, you may want to try to address it head-on. That might mean having a conversation with your boss about setting work boundaries or admitting to your partner how much you need and crave their encouragement. Of course, sometimes these efforts will be insufficient. While you cannot always change the opinions of others, you *can* be aware of whose opinion you want to take seriously and whose opinion you can let go of as you pursue your goals.

Everyday Distractions

Finally, there are many small everyday distractions that can derail us on a daily basis. Although these are usually little intrusions, over time they erode our progress toward our biggest hopes and dreams. Because these tiny interruptions incrementally chip away at our ability to fulfill our desires, it can sometimes take a long time for us to notice how much of a hindrance they are.

Here are just a few examples of common distractions, but there are many more:

- Email
- Texting
- Social media
- Binge-watching TV

Reflecting on your own life, ask yourself the following:

- Which distractions most commonly get in my way?
- Which distractions are easiest to handle?
- Which distractions feel most problematic to me?

Noticing when you lose out to these distractions is the first step to getting back on track.

Resources to Stay on Track

Although we will face hurdles to realizing our life audit, thankfully, there are many resources available to us to make things easier. Depending on the size and scope of your desires, along with other competing priorities and personal roadblocks in your life, you may find the following resources helpful:

PEOPLE

- A babysitter, caretaker, or school for your child so you can attend that weekly language class

- A partner who can take on more household chores so you have more time to pursue your dreams

- A parent who embodies and reminds you of your core values

- A friend who expresses interest and enthusiasm for your dreams

- A boss who encourages you to grow and take on bigger work goals that are aligned with your life audit

- A teacher who can troubleshoot questions with you and point you to other resources

- A mentor who can share their experience and lessons learned

PLACES

- A quiet space for deep thinking, creative pursuits, and exploring new skills or desires

- A coworking space, artist studio, or other dedicated area to commit to your goal

- A borrowed apartment, room, or office space

THINGS

- A calendar, journal, planner, timer, or other system to track your pursuits and keep you accountable

- An online community, newsletter, or chat board that plugs you into the community you aspire to be a part of

- A podcast about the subject or mechanics of what you are trying to accomplish

EXPERIENCES

- A class to teach you the basics of script writing, programming, podcasting, or whatever you need so you can make that career change

- Anything that fills your cup and inspires you, be it art or music, exploring nature, reading a good book, a conversation with a dear friend, baking or cooking, or a dance break with your kiddo

Although we can feel proud of ourselves for doing things on our own, don't shy away from using resources to reach your goal. There's nothing wrong with taking an assist to fulfill your wishes. The payoff doesn't come from how much you suffered in your journey or whether or not you did it all on your own. The payoff comes from tuning into yourself, working toward your goals, and making them real. Even those of us who are naturally inclined to be optimistic, have plenty of self-motivation, and know how to create our own momentum can benefit from a helping hand or word of encouragement. Use and embrace the tools you need to do this. Find what works for you and lean into it.

Stay Motivated

For many of us, our motivation is often highest at the beginning of a project—when we are in the blue skies, dreaming big, anything-is-possible phase. To keep your motivation high despite possible setbacks, try the following tactics.

GET QUICK WINS

Especially at the start of pursuing your goals, it's important to establish momentum. The best way to create momentum is to get quick wins—wins that help build confidence in your abilities and propel you forward into the next phase. To get a quick win, try the following:

- **Break up any elaborate goals into several smaller, more achievable ones.** (You can explore this on a weekly timeline, as we did before, or using other time frames. Make the first few steps simple enough so that you can guarantee you will be able to achieve them.)

- **Avoid burnout by pacing yourself.**

- **Plan for rest periods.**

- **Use each win as an opportunity to move the ball forward.**

For example, instead of committing to "get better at drawing," break it down into substeps: research drawing classes, check costs and registration dates, get necessary materials, and so on. Break the very first few steps into even smaller ones, such as "decide whether to attend an in-person or virtual class" or "choose which store you'll buy your materials from." Give yourself sufficient time to reach your goals. You might only need a few minutes to pick a store but a few weeks to choose the right class plus a few months of classes to see improvement in your drawing skills. If a yearlong commitment to a wish seems daunting, experiment with shorter versions (such as daylong workshops, eight-week weekly sessions, or a four-month semester of night classes) before committing to the Big Kahuna version of your goal (like getting your Master of Fine Arts degree). Use each quick win as proof that you are capable of doing more.

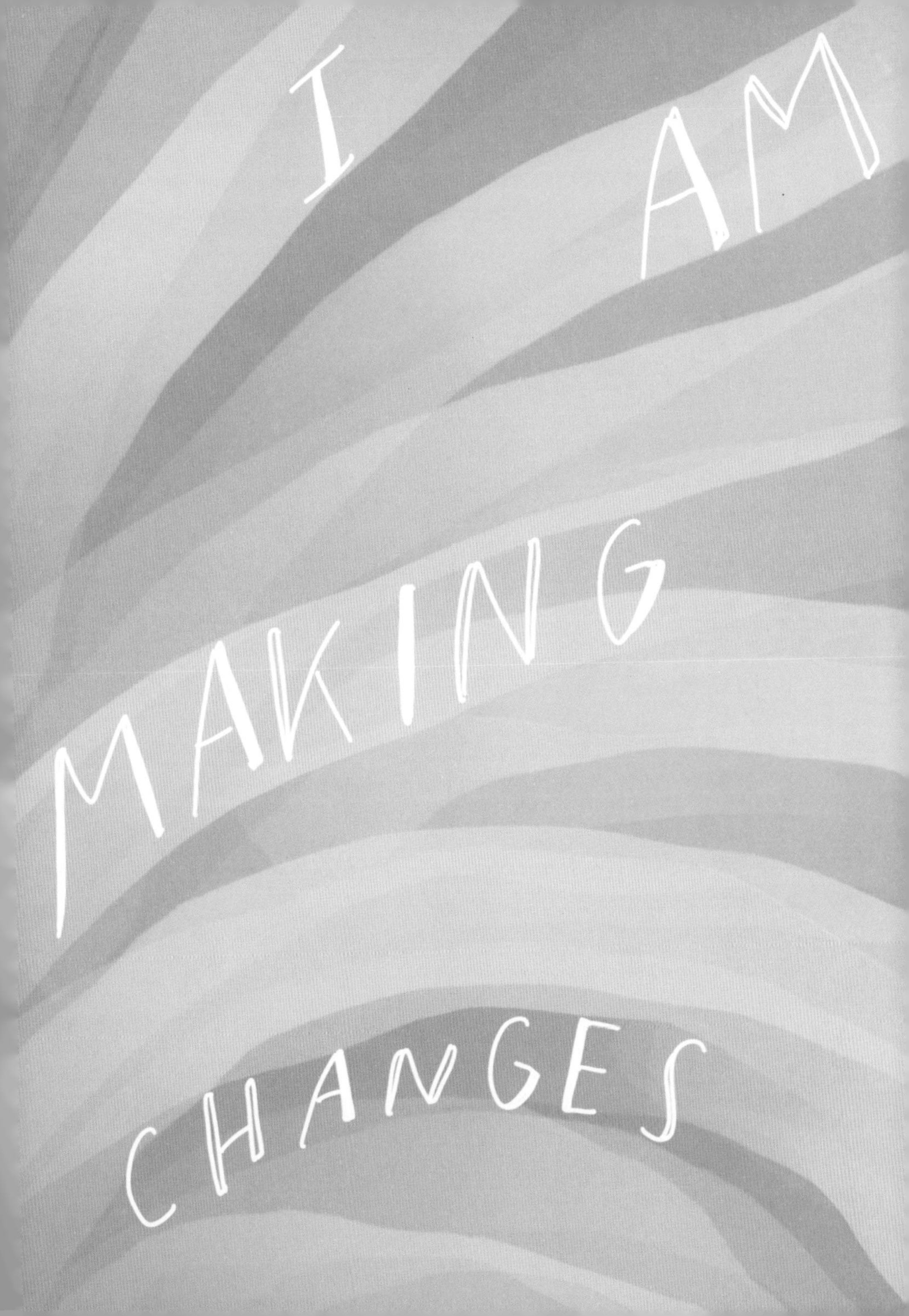
I AM
MAKING
CHANGES

BUILD SUPPORTIVE HABITS

Good habits can help us reach our goals faster. For example, if one of your values is to connect with your family more regularly, you can build a habit around it, like having regular family dinners on the calendar or virtual reunions if you're scattered across the country. You can also crush bad habits that regularly get in the way of reaching your goal, such as being glued to your device when you are with your partner or working so late you miss dinner with your kids. Consider these questions:

- Which habits do I have that already support my goals?

- Which bad habits should I be cognizant of?

- Are there any new habits that might accelerate my progress in reaching my goals?

Best Practices for Building Better Habits

Forming a new habit—or breaking an old one—can be challenging. (Hello, New Year's resolutions past.) Here is how to set yourself up for success:

1. **GET SPECIFIC.** Let's say you have a wish to bring more creative energy into your life. This ten-thousand-foot view is a useful start, but to make the most of it, you need to get specific. That might sound like: "I will go to one museum exhibition a month," or "I will freewrite for 15 minutes every morning after breakfast," or "I will sign up for an eight-week improv class." When we take the spirit of the intention and make it specific, we can more easily make progress.

2. **PAIR IT.** A pairing technique can help you get and stay motivated. This is especially helpful for stretch goals that may be meaningful but difficult to achieve. Say you wish to incorporate more movement into your life but you are not by nature a gymgoer or athletic type. By pairing something you already love with something you are learning to love, you begin to build a positive association with both. Limiting the activity you love (watching reality TV) to something you only do in combination with your stretch activity (working out) can be especially effective.

3. **ADD A VISUAL CUE.** Visual cues are clear, tangible reminders of what you have set out to accomplish. For example, if your goal is to prioritize rest, you can put a good book and your favorite pajamas on your bed an hour before you turn in. Your bedtime accessories act as a cue to get cozy and go to sleep, rather than watch another episode on Netflix. Visual cues that introduce convenience into routine are especially powerful.

TRACK YOUR PROGRESS

In our fast-paced, to-do-list-oriented society, many of us struggle to slow down, appreciate our progress, and bask in our own successes. Yet tracking our progress can be a powerful tool for seeing things through. It doesn't have to be as formal as keeping a daily log of your efforts (although it could be, if that's your speed). Tracking your progress could look like any of the following:

- Noticing how far you've come since you started working toward your goal

- Expressing gratitude for the people, places, and things that have helped you make progress as well as the hidden skills and talents you are discovering about yourself

- Realizing you've reached a new level of expertise, skill, or understanding

- Keeping a spreadsheet of the time you've spent fulfilling this wish

- Putting a thumbtack on a map of the world every time you travel someplace new

- Deepening your babysitting bench so that you can go on more date nights with your spouse

- Being able to walk a few miles without foot pain

- Whatever progress means to *you*

HOW DO you LIKE to TRACK youR PROGRESS?

TO-DO LIST

MONTHLY
PLANNER

STEPS in a
Day

FEELING
MORE CONNECTED
to youR PARTNER

RECORDING a
PODCAST EPISODE
on youR own

SHARPENING
KNIVES without
getting HURT

cutting
youR KIDS
HAIR without
NEEDING A
touch-up
LATER

CELEBRATE

However you track your progress, take a minute not just to notice it but to appreciate it as well. You have put in the time, energy, and focus to turn a wish into reality, and it is working. Celebrating might look like any of the following:

- Taking yourself out for ice cream, even in the dead of winter, for turning in your manuscript

- Framing a piece of your art you finally feel is good enough to hang on the wall

- Journaling about your achievement

- Sharing your progress with family and friends who celebrate you

- Dressing up as a small way of celebrating yourself

- Keeping an accomplishments box (see opposite page)

How do you like to celebrate yourself? Who or what makes you feel celebrated?

Keep an Accomplishments Box

If you prefer a more tangible way of celebrating, an accomplishments box can help. An accomplishments box is a physical place to track and store your wins. In writing down your accomplishments and revisiting them later, you get a double dose of good spirits and satisfaction. Here's how to do it:

1. **JOT IT DOWN.** Whenever you do something you are proud of, write it down on a piece of paper and put it in your accomplishments box, whether it's getting promoted, solving a personal medical mystery, reducing your screen time, or falling in love. Limit yourself to one accomplishment per sticky note, index card, or paper so that you can physically see your impact. You can do this for any accomplishment—not just life audit ones.

2. **KEEP IT OUT IN THE OPEN.** The first time I created an accomplishments box, I stored it under my bed (it wasn't a very nice box). But I realized that I was missing out. I could have savored more moments of enjoyment had I chosen a nicer box (or other container) and kept it out in the open. Pick a decorative box or decorate your own and keep it somewhere visible as a reminder of all your efforts and achievements.

3. **STAY CONNECTED TO YOUR ACCOMPLISHMENTS.** Make a point of regularly returning to your accomplishments box. Do this monthly or as a matter of routine, or simply take a peek inside every time you put a new card in the box. Open it when you need a confidence boost or are feeling down. You can also do an annual review to gear up for the next year's audit.

YOU ARE THE ARCHITECT OF YOUR LIFE

Stay Grounded in Your Purpose

I can still remember the day I ran my first life audit. It was unseasonably warm for a June afternoon in San Francisco, where the temperature generally hovers around 60 degrees no matter the month or season.

I remember wearing shorts and walking barefoot around my usually bustling apartment. My roommates were out of town, leaving the apartment blissfully quiet. The solitude was just what I needed: I was about to spend some time thinking about myself, my life, and where and how it was all going.

Nine months earlier, I'd taken a job I knew was not a forever job. I had moved across the country and started at a new company in a role I felt was not the best fit but a decent enough fit. I was trying to figure out what I wanted to do next. I was dating, making friends, and exploring a new city and a new side of myself. I felt open-minded, open-hearted, and eager for change. It was thrilling but confusing to feel pulled in so many directions. I had many questions about where to devote my time and energy but few answers.

The life audit would give me clarity, direction, and conviction in my values and purpose. It gave me focus and the courage to pursue a new career and to invest in my creativity. It reminded me day in and day out of the values I held dear, and it kept me in check when I veered offtrack.

Back then, my life audit felt instantly clarifying and gratifying, but even I had no idea how life-changing the experience would be. Ten years later, I return to the practice whenever I am feeling lost and unmoored or brimming with ideas I've yet to organize. It has gotten me through—or led me to—cross-country moves, career changes, relationship changes, and other adventures. I count on it to help me bring meaning, purpose, and clarity to my life, year after year. And now I'm extending it to you. It is your turn to make magic.

If you began this journey feeling overwhelmed by your ambitions, I hope you have found focus, intention, and the clarity and conviction in your pursuits, along with an action plan to make them happen. If you began these pages uncertain about the future, I hope you have some newfound certainty about what it is you truly want out of your one imperfect but beautiful life. If you have been seeking change, I hope the life audit has shined a light on how to make that change meaningful and fulfilling. With self-knowledge and focus, you can live your life with more intention, purpose, and clarity.

The end of your life audit is the beginning of a new chapter in your life. As you embark on this new phase, remember that when life gets confusing—when you begin to hear others' needs more than your own, or you feel pressured by societal expectations that may not align with your personal values—you have a grounding place to return to. Your life audit is a reminder of

I AM
THE
ARCHITECT OF
MY OWN
LIFE

what *you* hold dear—not what everyone else expects, wants, or needs from you.

You will, of course, have to make compromises over the course of your lifetime. We are not completely independent from our communities or our circumstances. You will need help from others, and they from you. But we needn't become codependent either. We needn't seek permission from others to pursue the things we know deep down will make us happy. If at times you begin to forget what it is *you* want—if the voices of others begin to crowd out your own inner wisdom, you can return to your life audit. Let it speak to you once more. Trust in what you have discovered about yourself, and let this guide your actions, behaviors, and decisions.

The changes you make won't happen overnight. You may want to change careers, start a family, travel the world, or live with more patience in your heart. Our ambitions for ourselves are nuanced and complex, and they involve not just our own drive and motivation but also the support and know-how of others. Look inward, but also look out toward your community for help in fulfilling your dreams.

Sometimes, things may feel beyond the scope of your abilities. You may wish to strike out on your own and be a solopreneur but lack the funds to do so. You may want to start a family but are still searching for your ideal partner. You may want to develop a rich social life outside of work but have a job that keeps you at your desk for long hours. If you hit a stumbling block, try to understand it. What change is needed? Is it you, or is it a broader system or culture that needs changing? What is one small thing you can do to move the needle in the right direction? Hurdles can derail us, but they can also be the seeds of change—individually and collectively.

When we make sense of our purpose and learn to live our lives with more intention and in alignment with our values, we make space for joy to enter our lives. We can move through the world with generosity of spirit and contentment toward others. We can be patient and at ease. We can be at peace.

As you ease into a life in line with your values and desires, remember to pay it forward. Practice empathy and understanding with those who are not yet living a purposeful life. Offer curiosity and encouragement for those still seeking to understand themselves. (You might even offer them a copy of this book or host your own group life audit session.) Make space for the people you love to go on a similar quest of self-discovery. Share your learnings in person or on social media (#lifeaudit). Be a gem.

Life ebbs and flows at its own rhythm. There is much that is out of our control. But when we are grounded in our own purpose, we can stay strong and rooted when life surprises us with new and unexpected challenges. We can stay calm and patient when it takes our tidy map and turns it upside down. When we know who we are and what we hold within us, life becomes a series of adventures to embrace rather than something to fear, freeze, or flee from. May you set forth on your life's journey with ease in your spirit and joy in your heart. May you remember why you're here.

Acknowledgments

My gratitude goes to everyone who read my original blog post on the life audit and inspired me to make it something bigger. Thank you also to the many life auditors who tested new prompts and helped me refine old ones.

Special thanks also to my agent, Leila Campoli; my editor, Rachel Hiles; my design counterpart, Wynne Au-Yeung; and everyone at Chronicle who had a hand in making this book come true.

Much love to my family, who've been there for me since the beginning. To Isaac and Elio, you are always in my audit.

FAQs

How do I know if I'm doing it right?

You're doing it right if you're being honest with yourself about what you want. There are no right or wrong answers about what that should look like. Take advantage of that! Write freely and without judgment: Don't think about what kinds of things are "right" to write about.

If you find you need to make modifications to the process to make it work for you, go for it. If you need to hit pause and come back to things, that's fine too. If you find yourself surprised or confused by what comes up for you, keep going—I promise clarity is on the other side. Your life audit is yours alone. You are doing it right as long as it is working for you.

Do I have to do my life audit alone?

You do not! Although I encourage privacy so you can really let those deepest desires see the light of day, many people find it energizing and motivating to conduct their life audit in the presence of others. You are free to conduct yours alone in your bedroom, on a friend retreat or trip, or even in a conference room with your colleagues. Just be careful not to let the presence of others influence you too much—the desires and wishes you come up with should be yours and yours alone. For this reason, it's best to work in silence for any brainstorming and reflecting. If you'd like to conduct your life audit in a group, decide up front whether you will simply be conducting life audits side by side or if you will share any of your self-discoveries with the group. While there are benefits to sharing with a group, such as getting advice on how to reach your goals or receiving validation from others with similar aspirations, I suggest sharing only if there is sufficient shared trust and intimacy in the group. Our dreams can be fragile this early in the process, and we don't want anyone derailing or influencing them. For more information on customizing your life audit for groups, please visit www.ximenavengoechea.com/the-life-audit.

Is it okay if I don't get through all my sticky notes?

Yes! One hundred is simply a target. Follow your heart and stop when you find you have nothing left to say.

Can I take a break or do I have to finish my life audit in one day?

Take as many breaks as you need! As the author of a book about rest (it's called *Rest Easy*), I am all about hitting pause and letting things marinate when necessary. There is no rush here. This is a process that requires introspection and deep contemplation, so if you sense your brain is turning to mush and you're not able to connect with that deeper inner wisdom, step back and take a break for a few hours or even a few days. But do return to it!

How much time will it take?

Your mileage may vary. The brainstorming part will only take an hour. Your analysis could take a few more. I recommend budgeting three hours from start to finish, at least for the first time you conduct your life audit. If you conduct your life audit more frequently after the first audit (say every year in time for the new year), the process will likely be much quicker. But it's nice to take your time, especially the first time around.

How do I make these changes stick?

Part 3 is for you, my friend! If you find yourself getting off-track, figure out why and determine what you can do about it by identifying your roadblocks, checking the resources you need to stay on track, and recommitting to the cause. Of course, if you find you are no longer invested in a change because you simply no longer feel connected to it, it's totally fine to deprioritize it. Interests change, and so do we. Just be sure that you are not nixing goals out of fear or insecurity.

How often should I conduct a life audit?

You can do this once or for the rest of your life. One benefit of conducting your life audit more than once is that you can see trends over time. For example, you can see how your interests might be changing or deepening as well as which hurdles are no longer in your way and what new challenges are cropping up. Because the life audit offers a clear snapshot of our thinking at a given moment in time, it can be very illuminating to return to it and see how our thinking and desires have changed over time. Milestone moments like the new year, your birthday, or the beginning of a new decade can be a great time to reflect and reset, and *The Life Audit* is the perfect companion for that.

Coming Soon:
The Life Audit Journal

If you've enjoyed your life audit process, you might enjoy
The Life Audit Journal, coming October 2025. In it, you'll find
meaningful prompts for self-assessment, self-discovery, and
self-actualization. It is the perfect companion to *The Life Audit*
book on your journey of self-discovery—a way to go even deeper
on what you've learned about yourself. *The Life Audit Journal*
guides you toward introspection and offers a beautiful space
to safeguard your thoughts and desires. With *The Life Audit
Journal*, you can return to your self-reflections and review them
or reflect on your progress (or on how much you've changed!)
as often as you'd like. Sign up at www.ximena.substack.com to
learn more about when it will be available.

Notes

Page 45, **Notes from the Field:**
Ximena Vengoechea, "7 Tips
for Running a Successful Team
Brainstorm—Even When Everyone's Remote," *The Muse*, last
modified May 5, 2023, https://
www.themuse.com/advice/remote
-brainstorm-tips.

Page 72, **According to many
motivational speakers and entrepreneurs:** Leo Widrich, "How the
People around You Affect Personal
Success," *Life Hacker*, July 16, 2012,
http://lifehacker.com/5926309/how
-the-people-around-you-affect
-personal-success.

Page 73, **How we spend our days:**
Annie Dillard, *The Writing Life*
(New York: Harper Perennial,
2013).

Page 141, **Many of us dislike
deadlines:** Christian Jarrett, "How
to Make Deadlines Motivating,
Not Stressful," *BBC*, April 10, 2020,
https://www.bbc.com/worklife
/article/20200409-how-to-make
-deadlines-motivating-not-stressful.

Page 165, **Cheat Sheet:** I outline
this concept in more detail in an
article I previously wrote for *Fast
Company*. Ximena Vengoechea,
"Why You Should Keep an
Accomplishments Box," *Fast
Company*, March 31, 2015, https://
www.fastcompany.com/3044480
/why-you-should-keep-an
-accomplishments-box.